The Green Guide for Historic Buildings

How to improve the environmental performance of listed and historic buildings

Published by The Stationery Office for

THE PRINCE'S REGENERATION TRUST

TSO
information & publishing solutions

Published by TSO (The Stationery Office)
and available from:

Online
www.tsoshop.co.uk

Mail, Telephone, Fax & E-mail
TSO
PO Box 29, Norwich, NR3 1GN
Telephone orders/General enquiries: 0870 600 5522
Fax orders: 0870 600 5533
E-mail: customer.services@tso.co.uk
Textphone 0870 240 3701

TSO@Blackwell and other Accredited Agents

Customers can also order publications from:
TSO Ireland
16 Arthur Street, Belfast BT1 4GD
Tel 028 9023 8451 Fax 028 9023 5401

First published March 2010

ISBN 9780117068445

Printed in the United Kingdom by The Stationery Office
P002343728 C10 03/10

Printed on 100% FSC Recycled material

Recycled
Supporting responsible use of forest resources
www.fsc.org Cert no. TT-COC-002625
©1996 Forest Stewardship Council
FSC

CLARENCE HOUSE

We are exceptionally fortunate to have so many wonderful heritage buildings in the United Kingdom; they provide the backdrop to our daily lives, connecting us to places and communities, our past and our future. Indeed, it is my belief that the entire fabric of society is closely interwoven with that of our built environment.

We would be wise, therefore, to look after these buildings very carefully and to neglect them at our peril. It is a real tragedy when we see them abandoned, derelict or destroyed. This, of course, is not only a terrible waste of resources, but a great missed opportunity.

My Regeneration Trust exists to find solutions for important historic sites when they are no longer needed for their original purpose, thereby helping to deliver heritage-led regeneration and breathing new life and vitality into deprived areas.

By bringing these buildings back into use we can capture the social and cultural energy, as well as the carbon which has been invested in them, often over hundreds of years. Crucially, re-use can be a catalyst for rejuvenating areas of social and economic need, providing jobs, homes and a high quality environment. For me, this is genuine sustainability.

This guide makes a small, but important contribution to the sustainability agenda. It is an example of true 'joined-up thinking', drawing together two areas that are particularly close to my heart - firstly, the careful stewardship of the U.K.'s rich heritage and, secondly, the need to protect the environment, including taking urgent action to avert the climate change crisis. Many people believe that these goals are in conflict; that old buildings leak energy through their windows, rooves and walls and are bad for the environment, so cannot be re-used sustainably. This guide seeks to dispel that, and other myths. In fact, the solutions for our listed buildings and our environment both lie in working with the grain of Nature.

I firmly believe that this guide will enable all those who care about the environment in which they live to navigate what can be a complex and technical subject and empower them to find the right long-term solutions for their important historic buildings.

I am so grateful to all those who have helped to fund this project. Their support has been invaluable in helping my Regeneration Trust reach out to a wide audience, and to share its expertise from more than a decade working on heritage-led regeneration projects.

CONTENTS

CASE STUDIES

FIGURES

TABLES

CHAPTER 1: Introduction

It is now widely accepted that human activity is causing our climate to change. Growing emissions of greenhouse gases like methane and carbon dioxide mean that global temperatures are rising, and rising sea levels are expected to follow.

In the UK, we can expect more extreme weather – such as flooding, heat waves and heavy downpours. The worst impacts, though, will be borne by countries in the developing world, who are least able to cope with them. This is why we must now take action on two fronts: firstly, to reduce our greenhouse gas emissions in order to minimise future climate change; and secondly, to learn to cope with the impacts of climate change that are now inevitable.

As political momentum, media interest and public awareness have increased, the body of legislation and targets for tackling climate change in the UK has grown quickly and substantially – perhaps most notably, the UK is committed to reducing carbon dioxide (CO_2) emissions by 80% by 2050. Meanwhile, energy is becoming more and more expensive, increasing by an average of 16% year on year between 2004 and 2008.[1]

The UK's buildings (our 'built environment') accounts for around 44 – 48% of the UK's carbon emissions.[2] We must make the buildings in which we live, work and spend our leisure time more energy efficient, and more capable of withstanding changing weather patterns. Although much of the effort so far has been focused on new build, buildings which exist now will comprise around 70% of the UK's total building stock in 2050.[3] They are therefore crucial to our efforts to tackle climate change, although they tend to be more difficult to address.

The picture for buildings which are listed as being of special historic or architectural interest, or are located in conservation areas, is particularly complicated: statutory requirements restrict what alterations may be made, so that they retain their features of special significance. This raises the question of whether they can be adapted in such a way as to minimise their greenhouse gas emissions and cope with a changing climate, whilst meeting legal constraints aimed at preserving their historic character.

The Prince's Regeneration Trust believes that the answer to this question is 'yes'. There is already evidence that it is nearly always preferable, in climate change terms, to re-use listed buildings than to demolish them: this saves energy and avoids waste.[4] Indeed, many were built at a time when energy was relatively more expensive and often have energy-efficient features and design.

To realise the full benefits of listed buildings for future generations, we must now identify ways to further enhance their environmental performance, working with the grain of individual buildings and using their original features as assets and pointers rather than obstacles to be overcome.

[1] 'The UK Low Carbon Transition Plan', p. 6 and p. 99.
[2] 'Retrofitting Soho', p. 12.
[3] Presentation by Hergen Hay at Ecobuild 2009.
[4] See, for example, 'Value Added: the economic, social and environmental benefits from creating incentives for the repair, maintenance and use of historic buildings'; and 'Lose or Re-use, Age Energy Research: a study of the energy usage of buildings relative to their age'.

In the broader sustainability context, listed buildings frequently play a very important role in the creation of strong, vibrant local communities and economies: they make a key contribution to our sense of place and cultural identity. Focusing on improving their environmental performance will ensure that they continue to be wonderful and viable places to live and work, well into the future. Indeed it may be obligatory: for instance, English Heritage already considers the environmental impact of all planning applications on which they are consulted (i.e. principally all applications relating to Grade I and Grade II* listed buildings). Similarly the Heritage Lottery Fund requires the projects it funds to include proposals for energy saving and microgeneration.

Many of the measures will save money over time, particularly as energy becomes more expensive. They should also improve comfort levels in the building for the benefit of all users (helping, for example, to tackle fuel poverty).[5] Above all, they will enable the conservation and relevance of our heritage well into the future.

We hope that this practical guide will help those who own and work on listed buildings to make successful environmental adaptations. Drawing on research studies and real-life examples, it sets out principles for deciding which measures are appropriate and effective for your building (and which are not), identifies common pitfalls to avoid, and illustrates this advice with best-practice examples.

[5] A household is considered to be in fuel poverty when over 10% of its income is needed to heat the home to satisfactory levels (deemed to be 21°C in the main living area and 18°C for other occupied rooms).

CHAPTER 2: About the guide

AUDIENCE

The guide is aimed at anyone seeking to refurbish, restore or re-use a listed building. It is intended to be accessible to all, regardless of whether or not you have previous experience in the fields of heritage or climate change.

> *Although the guide focuses very much on listed buildings, it applies equally to buildings in conservation areas and, in many cases, to unlisted older buildings. It is, of course, extremely important that other existing buildings and new buildings are also made sustainable, although that is beyond the scope of this guide.*

PURPOSE

The guide provides advice on what adaptations are likely to be appropriate for various listed buildings and how effective they are likely to be in saving money and carbon.

It is important to remember that each building is different and decisions about statutorily protected buildings must be made on a case-by-case basis. Therefore, you will still need to consult heritage specialists and the relevant local planning authority (which will be the final arbiter of this).

Likewise, where funding is being sought, it is important to ensure that you comply with the specific requirements and guidance relating to that funding source rather than relying purely on the information contained in this guide.

SCOPE

There are various definitions of sustainability, but the World Commission on the Environment and Development (also known as the Brundtland Commission) has defined sustainable development as:

"development that meets the needs of the present without compromising the ability of future generations to meet their own needs".

This guide focuses on the environmental performance of the final building and does not cover the sustainable re-use of the surrounding area or landscape, although this is also very important. It looks mainly at the environmental strand of sustainability and considers environmental issues falling into the categories of:

- greenhouse gas emissions;
- resource efficiency;
- adaptation to the impacts of climate change.

The Prince's Regeneration Trust is also committed to, and would strongly recommend to others, considering sustainability in the round, including wider environmental issues, along with social and economic impacts, such as the creation of sustainable communities, attractive places, long-term employment opportunities and economic wealth.

STRUCTURE

The guide begins by summarising key legislation and policy in the fields of both works to listed buildings and climate change and energy. The main body of the guide is then structured according to the order in which issues will be tackled during the process of taking on a listed building, identifying a use (or uses) for it, carrying out works to the building and, finally, beginning to use it.

The guide also identifies further sources of funding, information and expertise at Appendices A, B and C. A glossary of terms is provided at Appendix D.

CHAPTER 3: Statutory requirements, targets and policy

Since policy is changing all the time, it is important to refer to relevant up-to-date information sources (see the 'Useful links' section at Appendix C).

WORKS TO LISTED BUILDINGS

Planning controls apply in each part of the UK to ensure that works to listed buildings do not adversely affect their special architectural or historic interest (i.e. the reason why they were selected for listing).

You should consult heritage specialists and the local planning authority right from the beginning of the process and well in advance of carrying out works. There is also a range of statutory consultees whose views the planning authority will take into account when determining applications (e.g. The Society for the Protection of Ancient Buildings, The Victorian Society, The Georgian Group, The Twentieth Century Society, The Ancient Monuments Society, The Council for British Archaeology and Northern Ireland Environment Agency: Historic Buildings Unit).

It is a criminal offence to carry out works that affect the character of a listed building without the appropriate statutory consent.

Building regulations apply too, although some flexibility is allowed where listed buildings are concerned. It is also now obligatory (in England and Wales) to receive building regulations approval for any alterations affecting the energy use of a building.

Principles

The key principle is to avoid the unnecessary loss of significance, or special interest, which could derive from anything about the building, externally or internally.

For more guidance on conserving the significance of a building, please see The Prince's Regeneration Trust's guide on "How To: Write Conservation Reports".[6]

Before considering alterations it is important to understand the significance of the building and the potential impact these changes might have, whether it be to the plan-form, specific architectural details, old fabric or views of the building and how it relates to its neighbours. It is important to remember that the statutory protection applies to the whole building, not just the facades, or those features described in the written list entry.

[6] The guide is available from The Prince's Regeneration Trust's website: www.princes-regeneration.org

General underlying principles are to:

- consult the local planning authority at the earliest stage if you are considering carrying out any works;
- ensure you have enough information to properly understand the likely impact of your proposals upon the character and fabric of the building before undertaking any work;
- minimise the physical and visual impact of any work or new equipment, including by matching, blending and complementing the new with the old;
- avoid damage to significant historic fabric by intervening as little as possible to achieve the desired effect;
- ensure, as far as possible, that adaptations are reversible and will not compromise future use of the building;
- avoid removing fixtures, fittings or features of special historic interest, but, if this is unavoidable, and listed building consent has been obtained for the changes, photograph and record them in situ beforehand, and then store them carefully.

For churches that have Ecclesiastical Exemption, advice should be sought at an early stage from the appropriate Diocesan Advisory Committee (Anglican), Historic Churches Committee (Roman Catholic) or other denominational historic buildings committees.

Where previously unidentified historic features are uncovered during the course of building works, work should stop and the local planning authority should be contacted immediately.

You will need to consider the range of different options for improving environmental sustainability and be able to justify the ones you select, in both carbon and conservation terms, particularly if they have a greater impact than alternatives on the appearance or historic fabric of the building. Finding precedents nearby for the kind of work you are planning can be helpful.

Legislation and guidance

The most relevant legislation and guidance is listed below, for each part of the UK. Links to more detailed information can be found in the 'Useful links' section at Appendix C.

England and Wales

Planning (Listed Buildings and Conservation Areas) Act 1990

England only

Planning Policy Statement 15 and accompanying guidance (in draft at the time of writing, to replace Planning Policy Guidance 15 and 16)

Wales only

Circular 61/96; Planning Policy Wales (March 2002)

Scotland

Planning (Listed Buildings and Conservation Areas) (Scotland) Act 1997
The Historic Environment (Amendment) Scotland Bill (in draft at the time of writing)
Memorandum of Guidance on Listed Buildings and Conservation Areas 1998
National Planning Policy Guideline 18 Planning and the Historic Environment
Scottish Planning Policy 23 and the Historic Environment (also known as Scottish Historic Environment Policy (SHEP): Overarching Policy Statement on the historic environment)

Northern Ireland

Planning Policy Statement 6: Planning, Archaeology and the Built Heritage

Frequently asked questions: Getting Consents

Q ***When is listed building consent needed?***

Answer:

Listed building consent is required when a proposed change would affect the special architectural or historic character of the building. Any works that alter the building internally as well as externally could require listed building consent. To determine which works require consent and which do not, it is necessary to consult the conservation officer, or other planning officers, in your local authority, and it is essential to do this at an early stage.

In some cases, listed building consent might not be needed for measures such as pipework insulation, roof insulation, ground source heat pumps, water source heat pumps and ground-mounted solar panels. However, it is important always to check first with the conservation officer.

When is planning consent needed?

Answer:
Planning consent is required whenever you are materially altering the building, changing its use, sub-dividing or extending it. It is also required in certain other cases where additional planning controls apply.

Permitted development rights apply across the UK, allowing you to carry out some work without planning permission. They do not apply to listed buildings, and local authorities can also remove these rights on unlisted buildings, where they wish to preserve special character. Permitted development rights will be more restrictive in Conservation Areas, National Parks, Areas of Outstanding Natural Beauty or the Broads, and so planning permissions will more often be required.

Permitted development rights may allow you to install the following without planning permission (although you might still require listed building consent):

- roof-mounted solar thermal panels and solar photovoltaics which do not protrude more than 200mm beyond the plane of the wall or roof slope and are not visible from a highway;
- ground-mounted solar thermal panels or solar photovoltaics which are less than 4m tall, no closer than 5m to a boundary, have a surface area not exceeding $9m^2$ and are not visible from a highway;
- ground-source and water-source heat pumps, as long as all equipment is sited to minimise the impact on the building's appearance and the amenity of the area;
- flues which are no more than 1m above the highest point of the roof, not to be sited inside an Air Quality Management Area and are not on the principal elevation or visible from a road.

How do I get listed building and planning consents?

Answer:
After seeking pre-application advice from the conservation officer and planning officer, make two separate applications (for listed building consent and for planning consent). There will be a fee for planning consent but not normally a charge for listed building consent. You will need to provide drawings of an adequate scale and you will need to support the proposal with a written justification. In some cases a design or method statement may be needed to further explain how the works could be appropriate to the listed building.

When is conservation area consent needed and how do I get it?

Answer:
When it is proposed to carry out substantial demolition of a structure within a conservation area. Advice from the conservation officer is needed to agree what is judged to be substantial.

The procedure for obtaining conservation area consent is the same as for listed building consent (see above). There is no fee.

When is scheduled monument consent needed and how do I get it?

Answer:
Any works to a scheduled ancient monument require scheduled monument consent (unless permitted under the terms of the 1984 Class Consents Order).

To obtain scheduled monument consent you will need to apply to the relevant national heritage body (English Heritage, Cadw, Historic Scotland or the Northern Ireland Environment Agency). There is no fee.

When is building regulations approval needed and how do I get it?

Answer:
Most work to a building requires building regulations approval, including anything which affects the energy performance of the building.

After you have received the necessary listed building consent and planning consents, you will need to submit drawings to building control, which is part of the local planning authority. However, it is recommended to contact building control ahead of this to resolve any potential issues at an early stage in the design process. There is a fee for building regulations approval.

ENVIRONMENT / CLIMATE CHANGE

A range of statutory requirements, targets and policy goals have been put in place to tackle climate change, some of which focus on the built environment, which accounts for around 44 – 48% of the UK's carbon emissions.[7] These are summarised in Tables 5 – 9 for each part of the UK. Links to more information can be found in the 'Useful links' section at Appendix C.

! *It is important to remember that individual local authorities may also have their own guidelines on sustainability.*

[7] 'Retrofitting Soho', p. 12.

Figure 1: *Project process flowchart.*

This chart shows the main stages in a project from planning to putting the building into use.

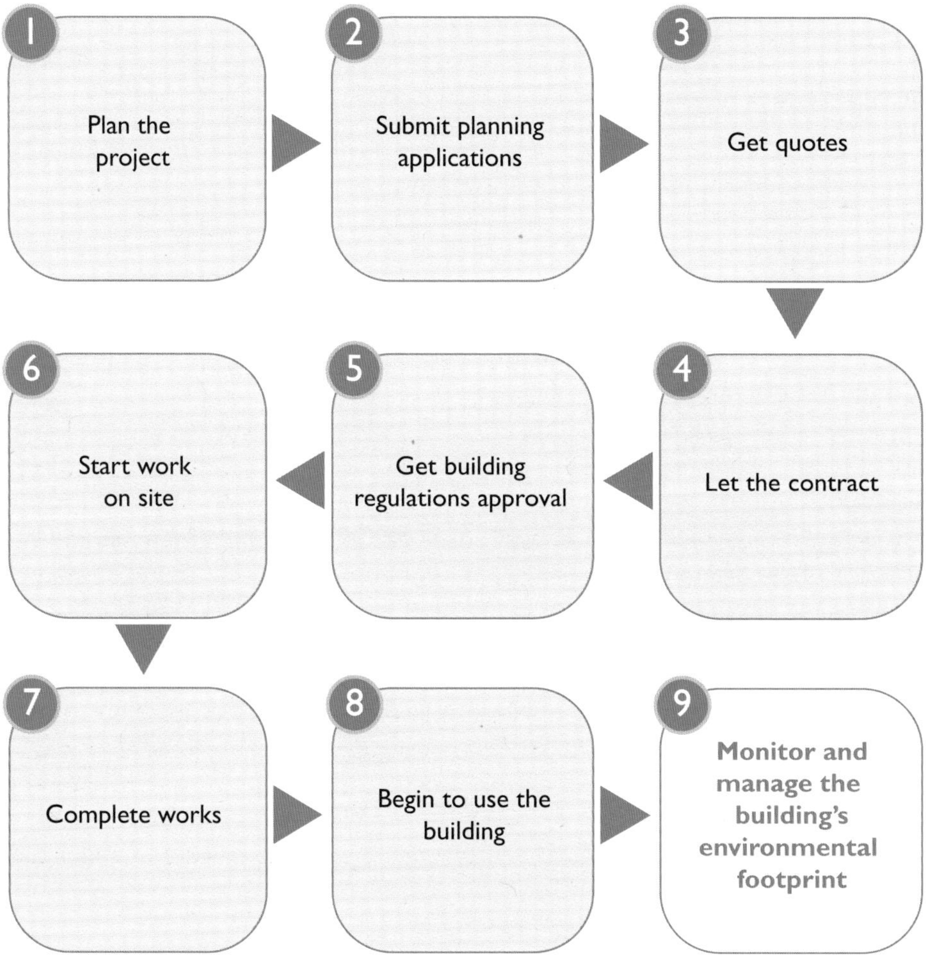

CHAPTER 4: Planning a sustainable project

The first step in improving the environmental performance of the listed building is to fully understand its original, current and proposed uses. Before starting to plan any work, you must think about:

- how it was intended to perform;
- how it actually performs; and, crucially,
- what are its special features of significance which must be conserved.

This will help avoid inappropriate or ineffective adaptations and, in many cases, it will direct you to measures which are most suitable.

> ! *The importance of developing this understanding must not be underestimated - it underpins the success of the whole project.*

MAKING THE MOST OF THE BUILDING'S DESIGN

Start by identifying the environmental assets of the building. For example, although traditional buildings may have relatively poor 'U-values' (i.e. heat is lost or gained through the fabric relatively quickly) they very often have a high 'thermal mass', meaning that they absorb and store warm or cool air, and are able to release it later.

Buildings with high thermal mass are good at naturally regulating the inside temperature, making the space warmer at night in the winter and cooler during the day in the summer. A US study shows that 'heavyweight' buildings can save up to 18% on the energy required for heating and cooling 'lightweight' buildings.[8] An Australian study found that this could be even greater, at up to 25%.[9] This will, of course, vary according to, for example, the insulation standard, access to sunlight and occupancy patterns.

The building may have relatively large south-facing windows, which allow the space inside to be heated naturally by sunlight ('passive solar gain'). Ensuring there are no obstacles to the light entering can reduce heating requirements in the winter. However, take care to avoid overheating in the summer, particularly as temperatures may rise in coming years (see Chapter 7 on adaptation to the impacts of climate change). Also remember that historic contents need to be protected from direct sunlight.

Most churches are aligned East / West so tend to have south-facing windows and roofs. This offers good opportunities for maximising passive solar gain and, possibly, generating power from sunlight, where this is done sensitively.

[8] 'Thermal Mass Energy Savings Potential in Residential Buildings', Conclusions section.
[9] 'Thermal Mass Sustainable Energy INFO fact sheet', p. 1.

The building will often be constructed using materials which have been sourced locally and are naturally less energy intensive, e.g. stone, lime mortar, timber and thatch. The existing materials can and should be re-used wherever possible, and close matches found for any new work. This is in line with both the conservation of the heritage and the environment. (For more detail, see the section on 'Building materials' on page **46.**

Similarly, the design and materials of the building may allow air to flow through naturally – natural ventilation – avoiding the need for mechanical ventilation, which consumes energy. Sometimes (especially as part of larger refurbishment projects) original design features of listed buildings can be used, or adapted, to channel air more effectively as part of a system of natural ventilation. For instance, chimneys can be used to create a 'stack effect' (for 'passive stack' ventilation) whereby the air inside is drawn through the building and displaced by cooler, fresher air from outside. Windows, vents, interior ventilation courts, rooftop ventilators, flues, cupolas in stairwells and halls, skylights and clerestories can help achieve effective natural ventilation. For an example of how natural ventilation can be used effectively, see the following case study on the Government Offices.

Hints and tips

Think about what is needed to bring the building back in to good condition and remember that repair and maintenance is more environmentally sustainable than carrying out extensive and intrusive work.

Chimneys are a good source of natural ventilation

CASE STUDY: Government Offices, Great George Street, London

This Grade II* listed building was designed and built between 1898 and 1917. The principal architect was John Brydon, with Sir Henry Tanner taking over after Brydon's death. It was constructed in two phases, with the Parliament Street end completed in 1908 and the St James' Park end built between 1910 and 1917. It has housed a number of public offices and departments. During World War 2 the basement was famously used for the Cabinet War Rooms. The building is now occupied by HM Treasury, HM Revenue and Customs and The Cabinet War Rooms museum.

Interior view of HM Treasury Building: light-wells used for ventilation

HM Treasury Building, Great George Street, London

The refurbishment, which began in 1999, made use of several larger lightwells, covering them with inflatable roofing made from ETFE, a transparent, recyclable foil.

This created light, pleasant meeting places, cafes, libraries and reception areas. These are also an essential element of the ventilation system: fresh air is drawn into the building through windows at the office perimeters and the lightwells form thermal chimneys in which stale air from office spaces rises, due to the stack effect, and is discharged through integral louvred vents at roof level. The louvres are linked to weather stations on the roof so they respond automatically to weather changes. This means that the building is largely naturally ventilated, with just a small amount of mechanical ventilation used in commonly used spaces, such as meeting rooms, restaurants and areas affected by traffic noise.

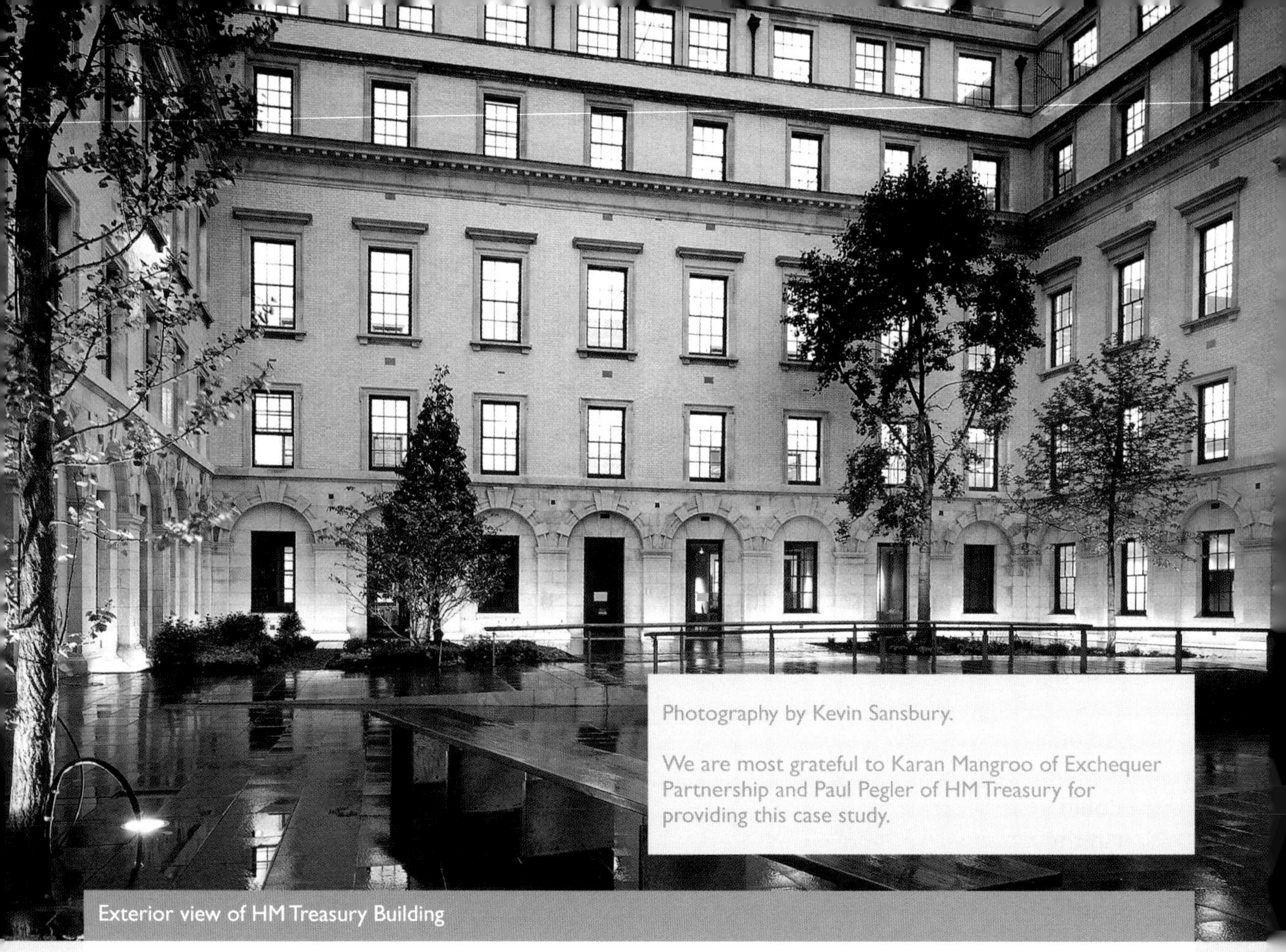

Photography by Kevin Sansbury.

We are most grateful to Karan Mangroo of Exchequer Partnership and Paul Pegler of HM Treasury for providing this case study.

Exterior view of HM Treasury Building

Substantial efforts have been made to achieve 'excellent' and 'very good' BREEAM ratings, with full marks for ventilation (along with lighting control and thermal comfort). During refurbishment 92% of original timber from windows was re-used, and 70% of floor timber, with all procured timbers from suppliers accredited by the Forest Stewardship Council. Eighty-eight percent of building waste was recycled.

Windows were replaced with a laminated single pane 'sandwich' incorporating a UV-filter safety film to reduce glare and heat gain in normal usage, and avoid splintering in the event of breakage. Each sash window was re-beaded to retain the integrity of the original design.

The building is carefully managed and accredited to ISO14001 Environmental Management System standard, with regular reviews undertaken by professional bodies such as the Carbon Trust. Some of the initial and recent initiatives included installation of 11,000 low energy, long-life bulbs, installation of metering for better utilities usage monitoring and changing office cleaning from night to day for more efficient energy management.

A commitment to sustainability means that both the building managers and the building occupiers continuing to seek environmentally friendly solutions and set a good example for the rest of the government estate.

DATA GATHERING

As well as taking pointers from the design of the building, you should aim to gather as much data as possible at the beginning of the project on the actual environmental performance of the building.

First you should get a picture of energy and resource consumption of the building in use. This will provide an indication of where the biggest impacts can be made to improve environmental sustainability and save money. For instance, if most of the energy is needed for heating and cooling, then retrofitting a more efficient ventilation system may be most worthwhile, whilst if water demand is relatively high, water-saving fixtures and fittings, and possibly a rainwater harvesting or grey water system, might be a priority.

Some ideas for how to get the data are set out below:

- if there is a Display Energy Certificate for the building, this will tell you the actual energy usage of the building;
- analyse utility bills and meter readings;
- you could install a 'smart meter', which provides information about how much energy is being used in the building at different times during the day (and how much this is costing you);
- if the building is not currently being used (or not in the way that is anticipated in the future) it may be possible to find data from a building of similar size, design and use pattern;
- you may also be able to use computer modelling to estimate energy use.

It is also important to understand where the most energy is being wasted (e.g. through windows, walls, doors, the roof, the floor or inefficient fixtures and fittings). This will highlight areas to target your efforts to maximise environmental impact and cost-effectiveness. For instance, if you find that most of the energy is being lost through windows, fitting shutters, blinds, interlined curtains or secondary glazing should be investigated early on.

Each building will have different strengths and weaknesses, according to its design, composition and environment, so careful testing is important for maximising the effectiveness of environmentally sustainable measures and techniques.

Did you know: it is possible to lose 15% or more of heat through inadequately insulated pipes if there are long pipe runs in large buildings? Leaking underground pipes or dripping taps represent an unnecessary use of water and, where the water is being pumped around the building or heated, can result in wasted energy too.

Thermal image of Lauriston Place, Edinburgh. © City of Edinburgh Council. See pages 68 – 69 for the full case study.

Assessing wastage can be done through:

- thermal imaging (or thermography) which displays a map of the surface temperatures of different parts of a building. The images can show where insulation is missing, where draughts exist, or where there are problems with damp;

- fan pressure tests, which measure the air leakage from the building and determine the location and extent of the worst draughts, and, if necessary, compartment tests to isolate different parts of the building;

- dynamic thermal simulation, which can be used to assess thermal mass, temperature and humidity readings;

- devices fitted to the building's water systems to detect water leaks and wastage.

If you cannot carry out as thorough tests as you would like, these guidelines may help:

- Most heat loss from a building is through the walls and roof due to poor insulation, with a significant proportion also being lost through windows, floors and chimneys. 'Cold bridging' (also known as 'thermal bridging') occurs where areas of low heat resistance come into contact, allowing heat to flow through the path created.

- In general, walls where plaster has been applied directly are likely to let more heat through than walls with lath and plaster, which in turn waste more energy than walls with plasterboard. Therefore, wall insulation may be more important to consider for walls of the former construction types. However, dry-lining (i.e. a method of adding insulation to the inside of the wall) is not traditional and in certain buildings would look out of character. It will also require very careful installation to ensure adequate ventilation. For more information see Chapter 5 on reducing energy demand.

- To give a very rough estimate, the total energy one person spends on heating and cooling in any kind of building is 37 kilowatt hours per day (12 for hot water, 24 for hot air and 1 for cooling).[10] Meanwhile, an average two-bedroom household requires around 4,000 kilowatt hours of electricity per year.[11] However, these figures should be treated with caution – they are, of course, an average and each building and user will be different (especially, for example, if electricity rather than gas is used for heating).

- Naturally ventilated offices in existing buildings tend to use between 55 and 90 kilowatt hours of electricity per square metre of floor area per year, and around 145 kilowatt hours of gas. For offices with air conditioning, electricity use can be 225 – 360 kilowatt hours, with gas at around 175-200 kilowatt hours.

- Existing buildings used for retail tend to consume around 200 – 450 kilowatt hours[12] of energy per square metre per year.[13] The figure for industrial buildings is similar.

Hints and tips

It is important to carry out thermal imaging in the right environmental conditions, as factors like strong winds and rainfall can distort the results. You must also ensure that the emissivity of different surfaces is taken into account.

When carrying out fan pressure tests, it is not normally necessary to use an expensive calibrated fan for simple draught identification purposes; a less expensive fan should be sufficient.

Don't forget that some air circulation is needed to maintain the 'health' of traditional buildings, which were designed to 'breathe', and to provide sufficient air changes for the occupants.

It is important to continue to test the leakage of air from the building during and after the works, to ensure that they have the desired effect.

10. 'Sustainable Energy – Without the Hot Air', p. 53.
11. 'Feasibility Study on Torr Vale Mill', p. 26.
12. 'Transforming Existing Buildings: The Green Challenge Final Report', p. 3.
13. 'Transforming Existing Buildings: The Green Challenge Final Report', p. 9.

Figure 2: *Heat loss from a traditional flat.*
This chart shows the heat loss (Watts per Kelvin) and percentage contribution to space heating load of different building elements and process for a traditional flat.

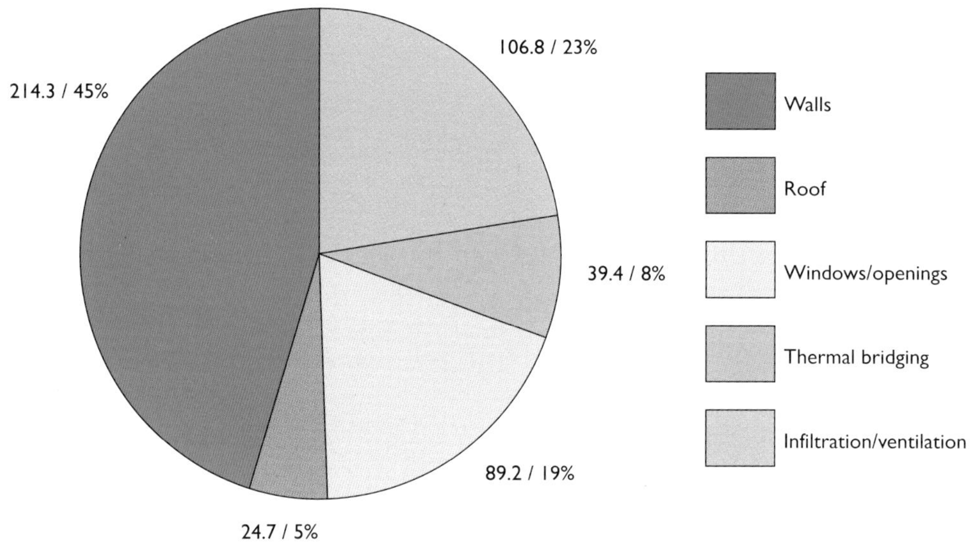

Figure 3: *Heat loss from a traditional cottage.*
This chart shows the heat loss (Watts per Kelvin) and percentage contribution to space heating load of different building elements and process for a traditional cottage.

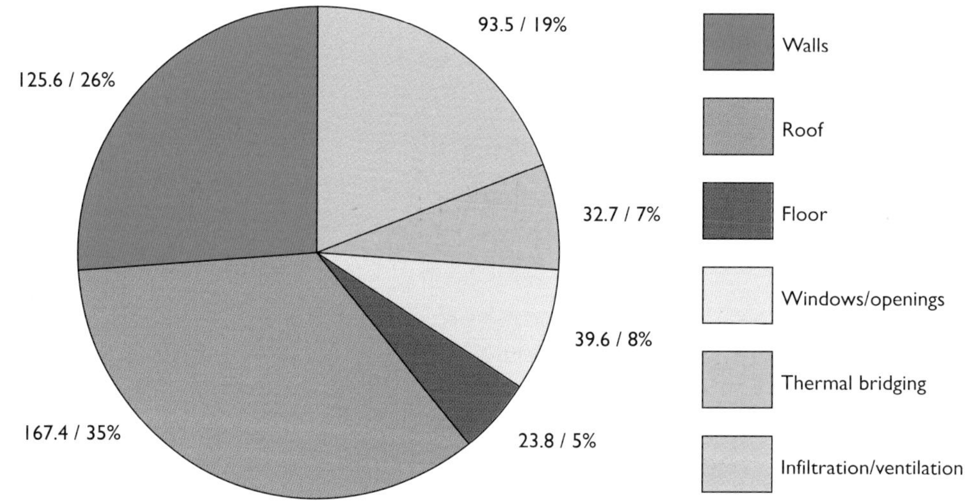

Figure 4: *Heat loss from a traditional detached house.*
This chart shows the heat loss (Watts per Kelvin) and percentage contribution to space heating load of different building elements and process for a traditional detached house.

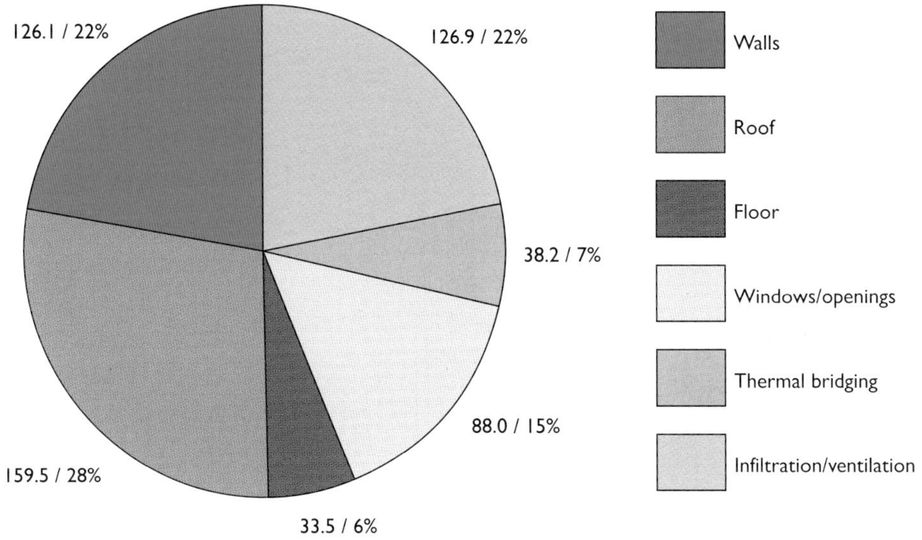

Charts reproduced from Energy Modelling In Traditional Scottish Houses.

FINDING A NEW USE

It is always better to keep a building in the use for which it was originally designed. However, where a building's original purpose has ceased, you should re-use it for a different purpose. Identifying a new use will depend on factors including:

- what is economically viable;
- what the owner or local community want and need;
- what can obtain approval from the local planning authority – i.e. what alterations are considered acceptable.

Where the building is sufficiently large to accommodate more than one type of use, combining various uses (e.g. for residential, commercial and community purposes) tends to be more environmentally – and economically – sustainable than just using it for one type of development. This is because it encourages people to get around by foot, rather than needing to travel in a car, or other fuel-powered vehicle. However, other buildings in the nearby area may already meet some of those needs, so it is important to take a holistic, area-based view.

Once the likely use of the building is known, you can begin to identify particular needs and patterns for energy and other resources at different times, and associated opportunities for reducing energy demand. Some issues to consider are discussed below.

- Buildings with relatively high thermal mass take longer to reach comfortable temperatures when it is either very hot or very cold outside, but will stay at the desired temperature for longer. Therefore, these kinds of buildings operate most energy efficiently when use is fairly constant, rather than, say, if a room is just needed for a couple of hours a day.

- If a building is mainly used when it is dark outside, solar photovoltaics and solar thermal panels may be less appropriate than other measures (although energy could be stored in batteries or exported to the grid).

- Where a building is being used sporadically, renewable technologies which generate electricity (that can be stored in batteries or returned to the grid when not needed) may be more appropriate than technologies which supply hot water, as it is not possible to store this energy for long periods of time.

- If some rooms will not be used during certain parts of the year, they could be closed off for that time, with heating kept to the minimum required to conserve the building fabric. Likewise, 'zones' could be created in the building where activities which require similar temperatures at similar times can be clustered. For instance, in commercial buildings, activities which need high levels of energy (e.g. cooling requirements for IT equipment) should be located in one place and separated from areas used for other activities, for maximum efficiency.

- Museum exhibits are likely to require control of relative humidity to between 50 and 60%. They should be enclosed wherever possible and appropriate so that the rest of the building need not be controlled to the same degree.

- In industrial buildings, around 80% of the energy used is operational (the energy used in running the building) rather than embodied (the energy used in constructing it). Therefore it is particularly important with these buildings to ensure that the day-to-day energy loss is minimised, especially that used for lighting, heating and cooling, which accounts for a large portion, and that it comes from sources which are as clean as possible (see Chapter 6 on moving to cleaner energy).

- Commercial operations tend to be far more carbon intensive than homes. The average energy consumption of the UK service sector is 30 watts per square metre per unit of floor area.[14] They use a much higher proportion of electricity from the grid, as opposed to gas (which has a smaller carbon footprint).[15] Therefore, it is a priority to reduce electricity demand here and maximise the proportion of electricity generated from renewable sources (see Chapter 6 on moving to cleaner energy).

[14] 'Sustainable Energy – Without the Hot Air', p. 298.
[15] 'Retrofitting Soho', p. 43.

- Think about the amount of variation in the use of a building over a typical day, or week. For instance, some commercial and industrial premises require large amounts of energy for a set portion of the day (e.g. for industrial processes, IT, lighting heating and cooling), whereas homes and some offices may not need the heating and cooling systems to respond so quickly. Underfloor heating systems, using e.g. biomass boilers and heat pumps, tend to be more suitable where there is lower variation in use, with air-based systems offering faster response times.

- In a mixed-use development (e.g. one that includes a mixture of residential and commercial buildings) heat produced by offices may be able to be captured during the day and used to meet the heating requirements of homes in the evening.

- The large amounts of energy used for IT in offices also make it particularly important that those working in the building switch off equipment when it is not needed.

Did you know: our workplaces are responsible for 20% of UK emissions?[16]

- Usually a larger proportion of energy is required for lighting in offices, and especially retail outlets, than in homes, so it is even more important to ensure that energy efficient-lighting options are installed here. However, lighting, appliances and cooking still account for around a quarter of energy use in the home, so switching to the most energy-efficient products can make a significant difference here too.[17]

- Homes tend to require more heating and hot water than workplaces (often accounting for more than 70-80% of energy consumption).[18] Hot water use (from washing, cooking, washing clothes and dishes and tumble-drying) can be around 12 kilowatt hours per day per person.[19] This is the equivalent of switching on a 60W light bulb for 200 hours. Therefore, water-heating technologies like solar thermal panels may be more useful here than in commercial premises. Since hot water will often be needed by more than one occupant at the same time, relatively bigger hot water tanks may be necessary in homes.

Chapter 8 returns to the issue of improving the environmental performance of the building in use. It looks at ways to live or work in a building, after work to convert it has been carried out, to minimise its overall environmental footprint.

16 'The UK Low Carbon Transition Plan', p. 12.
17 'Office of Climate Change Household Emissions Project', p. 5.
18 'Office of Climate Change Household Emissions Project', p. 5.
19 'Sustainable Energy - Without the Hot Air', p. 51.

IMPORTANT PRINCIPLES

For each environmental measure you consider, try to estimate the reduction in energy or resource use it will bring about over the lifetime of the building and compare this with the energy and resources required to produce, transport and install the raw materials involved. In most cases, the former will far exceed the latter – i.e. there is a net environmental benefit. However, if it does not then the measure is not justifiable on purely environmental grounds.

When costing out the work, don't forget to factor in additional costs, like undertaking technical drawings and feasibility studies, hiring a quantity surveyor and consulting a renewable energy design engineer for larger jobs, as well as carrying out quality checks.

For any work on listed buildings, it is most important always to use professionals and contractors with specialist expertise in heritage buildings. Careful design and execution will always be necessary to ensure a sensitive change is achieved.

It is also recommended to use companies that operate with regard for the environment – for instance, those certified with International Standard ISO14001.

CHAPTER 5: Reducing demand for energy and resources – the building fabric and contents

Before thinking about where energy will come from to power the building, it is always best practice first to minimise the use of energy and resources (e.g. water). Sometimes you can do both in tandem, for example if you plan to install a new, high-efficiency boiler, which could be linked to a renewable heating system. This is the most practical, cheap and efficient approach. Money spent, for example, on improving insulation will generally be more cost-effective than that spent on microgeneration and, in a listed building, creates far fewer design or conservation challenges. Equally, once the energy requirement is reduced, smaller renewable systems can be installed which are both cheaper and easier to accommodate.

Did you know: energy use accounted for three-quarters of global greenhouse gas emissions in the year 2000?[20]

It can be difficult to retrofit some energy-saving measures, and a major adaptation or enlargement project generally offers the best opportunities, at the lowest relative cost. Where modern extensions are planned, there should be even more scope to build to higher environmental specifications. It is also sometimes possible to retrofit less disruptive, or more targeted, measures for saving energy and resources where the building is undergoing more minor adaptation – even when it is still being occupied.

The general rule here is not to compromise key features of the listed building when savings in energy can be achieved through more reversible means.

Energy demand can be substantially reduced by making changes to the fabric of the building – e.g. its walls, roof, chimneys windows, doors and contents. However, great care must be taken when this is done to a listed building in order to avoid damaging its special character. In buildings of traditional construction, maintaining breathability, rather than sealing the building, is also crucial for avoiding condensation and damp. Therefore, when installing the measures discussed below it is important to work closely with the contractors and workforce to ensure they understand the aims of the project.

INSULATION

In new build, it is good practice to keep air leakage from the building below $3m^3/m^2/hr$, and certainly no more than $10m^3/m^2/hr$ (according to Part L of the Building Regulations). This aspiration may well not be appropriate for buildings of traditional construction: such buildings were designed to allow air to circulate and sealing them up can create problems of damp, timber decay and mould growth. Since survival of historic timber might be one of the reasons for the building being listed, protecting it from decay is particularly important.

[20] 'Sustainable Energy – Without the Hot Air', p. 16.

However, air leakage can often still be substantially and safely reduced, firstly through insulation. It may also be possible to take preventative steps when installing insulation; for example, by fitting a roof vent for ventilation – depending on whether this could be done without visual impact from key vantage points (e.g. through the use of perforated slate vents).

> *Partial insulation can sometimes be worse than no insulation at all, causing moisture build-up and damaging the fabric of the building. It is therefore important that a thorough, holistic approach is taken to insulating the 'building envelope'. This will help avoid 'cold bridging', where a cold spot is created in an area where new insulation meets an area with no insulation.*

Start by insulating pipework, valves, boilers, hot-water cylinders and cold-water tanks (but not the floor space below the tank). This is highly unlikely to raise any issues around visual impact or intervention to the historic fabric.

After that, roofs may be the next easiest target for insulation and this is also extremely cost-effective, reducing CO_2 emissions by nearly a quarter in some cases.[21]

> *If there are bats or birds in the roof you should take advice when carrying out any works, as all UK bats and some birds are protected by law.*[22]

For pitched roofs, insulation should be installed directly above the top floor ceiling, between ceiling joists, and on the underside of the roof; or, if the attic is used for further accommodation, the insulation should be only on the underside of the rafters. It may also be possible to apply insulation between the rafters, but this must be done very carefully to avoid mould developing between the insulation and the vapour-permeable membrane. It is important to insulate the loft hatch too. Loft insulation should be at least 250mm thick where possible. Research by Historic Scotland found that adding insulation improved the U-value of a pitched roof from 2.3 to 0.15W/m^{2}K.[23] It is important, though, to ensure adequate ventilation is maintained around the eaves, especially, to avoid moisture building up between the insulation and the roof slates.

Flat roofs are more difficult to insulate, but a continuous vapour control layer can be added above ceiling level, ensuring there are no breaks in the seal. External insulation may also be a cost-effective option for flat roofs.

In the case of thatched roofs, thatch is already a good insulator (unless, for instance, poor detailing means that excessive air movement is occurring), so further insulation may not be necessary, although a good standard of insulation at ceiling level is still important.

[21] 'Energy Modelling in Traditional Scottish Houses', p.19.
[22] More information is available from the Bat Conservation Trust and the RSPB. A joint publication, 'Bats in Traditional Buildings', by English Heritage, The National Trust and Natural England has also been published and is available to download from the HELM website (for further information see 'Useful links' section at Appendix C).
[23] 'Energy Modelling in Traditional Scottish Houses', p. 24.

Most listed buildings of traditional construction have solid walls, without cavities where insulation could be added. Solid masonry walls in an old building tend to have a U-value of around 2.4U, where U-values can be 0.6U or less for buildings built to modern standards or with insulated cavity walls.[24] Insulation of external, but not internal walls, is most complementary to buildings with high thermal mass but can be very costly and will not always be appropriate.

External overcladding, where insulation is added to the outside of the building, is almost always unacceptable because of its impact on the appearance of the building, the roof line, rainwater goods, window reveals and sills and doorways. It should probably only be considered where the facade is in such poor condition that it cannot be retained anyway.

Alternatively, internal insulation ('dry-lining') can be considered in certain cases, adding a layer of insulation on the inside of the walls. However, its carbon and thermal benefit needs to be considered against the potential loss of historic character through concealing old plasterwork or limewashed stone walls and the potential need to remove architectural detailing such as panelling and cornices. As a result, insulation of this kind is often inappropriate in listed buildings, although it may be possible in rooms with little or no detailing, or where complete replacement of plasterwork is being carried out. Remember that in general the thicker the original walls the less thermal benefit would be gained from this type of insulation. Meanwhile, the trapping of condensation between the external and internal surfaces can create serious long-term damp problems; it is very important to avoid this.

Floor insulation can be very effective too: in Grade B listed tenements in Edinburgh, the U-value of the concrete basement floor fell from 3.5U to 0.6U when insulation was added (see pages 68 – 69 for the full case study).

Floor finishes need to be lifted and relaid to install wall and floor insulation so, again, this may be more appropriate in cases where large-scale refurbishment is needed. You will need to seek specialist archaeological advice. Take particular care when lifting older, wide hardwood floorboards, or boards fitted with tongue-and-groove edges, both to ensure they are not damaged and because they can act as a structural element in historic buildings. Tongue-and-groove boarding prevents heat loss far better than butted floorboards, so there is an environmental argument for retaining them in situ if at all possible. Similarly, original fireproofing or sound deadening between joists may be of special historic interest and, if so, should be conserved. Again, insulation should be as thick as possible, for maximum energy efficiency, whilst avoiding the need to adjust significant skirtings, doors and sockets – a particular problem with solid floors.

It may be sensible to use thinner insulation where suspended timber floors already have a layer of 'deafening' material below the floorboards. Original floors of special historic interest (e.g. flagstones or decorative tiling) should not be covered. However, in certain circumstances, they can be carefully lifted, a limecrete floor laid and the historic flagstones or tiles relaid on top.

[24] 'Sustainable Energy – Without the Hot Air', p. 290.

Natural insulation materials

Again, be very careful when adding insulation to a listed building of traditional construction to ensure the fabric can still 'breathe'. A good way to achieve the necessary ventilation is through the use of natural insulation materials, including:

- cotton;
- hemp;
- flax;
- wood cellulose;
- sheep's or lambs' wool.

These absorb moisture and let it evaporate without impairing performance. Moreover, they have a low embodied energy (see the section on 'Building materials' on page 46 for more on this). Natural materials tend to be most appropriate for listed buildings. In contrast, human-made materials (like fibreglass and mineral wool) hold moisture – they are generally better suited to buildings designed to keep out moisture altogether, rather than allowing it in and out. However, they are significantly cheaper and can be used in some cases if installed, monitored and maintained very carefully.

Non-permeable materials (like foil-backed insulation, damp-proof membranes and glues) should be avoided altogether. Avoid spray-on insulation, as it can prevent proper inspection, hinder re-use of slates or tiles and reduce ventilation, as well as looking unsightly.

Installation of cladding and weather boarding

Berg Cottage, Barkway, Hertfordshire. All photographs reproduced courtesy of Oxley Conservation Limited

CASE STUDY: Berg Cottage, Barkway, Hertfordshire

Berg Cottage is a Grade II listed timber-framed, thatched cottage, owned by the National Trust but tenanted. Other than some thatching, the building had not been subject to significant repairs since the 1930s. It was cold and draughty and expensive to heat. Repair works in 2002/3 to rectify damage from well-intentioned but inappropriate works provided an opportunity to improve thermal comfort and energy efficiency.

A fan pressurisation test showed that, whilst little heat was escaping through windows, there was significant loss through the walls and the tiled slopes below the dormer windows. The tiles were lifted, and woodfibre board and vapour-permeable roofing felt was laid over the roof timbers and up under the thatch as far as possible. The verges of the thatch were repaired to ensure a good overlap with the tiles. This addressed a principal area of air leakage, which significantly improved the performance of the building.

The need to remove weatherboarding and cement render, for the purposes of repair, provided the opportunity to improve the performance of the leaky walls. The walls were insulated with sheep's wool between interior and external finishes so as to retain historic character.

The walls were re-rendered, with no vapour or secondary barriers installed between the timber frame and new render; this allows moisture to be temporarily absorbed and then released, an effect which is reinforced by the sheep's wool insulation. Re-cladding with vapour-permeable tongue-and-groove woodfibre board behind new weatherboarding improved insulation and acted as a wind barrier to reduce air infiltration and convection, whilst importantly adding thermal mass to the lightweight structure.

Fan pressurisation test at Berg Cottage

Similarly, vapour-permeable roofing felt and proprietary tape was dressed over the joints and around openings. This significantly increased the performance of the walls, again removing a significant source of draughts and associated discomfort to the tenants. Meanwhile, dampers were added to chimney flues to allow use but minimise heat loss when not in use.

Original windows were simply draught-stripped, except those which no longer fitted sufficiently well, where secondary glazing was installed.

Installing wall insulation at Berg Cottage

The refurbishment reduced CO_2 emissions by three tonnes per annum from 11.1 to 8.1 tonnes. Gas consumption fell by 27%.

Using a fan pressurisation test before and during the works was crucial: it showed that the building actually became more leaky at first and allowed troubleshooting of problems to ensure the heat loss was eventually reduced.

We are most grateful to Richard Oxley of Oxley Conservation Ltd, and The National Trust, for providing this case study.

DRAUGHT-PROOFING AND WEATHER-STRIPPING

First of all make sure windows and doors fit well, as large amounts of heat are often lost through poorly fitting windows. Over time, windows do need overhauling, and this can provide the opportunity to add weather-stripping. With timber windows this can be done relatively cheaply through complete overhaul and sometimes the addition of carefully inserted brushes into the window frame, for example to act as a seal between the upper and lower window frame. Sash windows in particular can be easily removed and rehung using this method, although care needs to be taken to ensure that especially important windows are not altered. The process usually involves the replacement of timber beading (staff and parting beads), but this is more acceptable than insertion of a wholly new window. A growing number of window repairers know how to carry out this kind of simple and effective overhaul (which used to be common practice but which died out with the mid-20th century shift to side-opening windows). Overhauling sash windows makes them easier to use and so also encourages proper ventilation.

When draught-proofing around windows, surface-mounted rubber seals should be avoided as they detract from the appearance of the window and are less effective than brushes. Metal windows can have a rubber seal injected into the space between window and frame but, again, often the most effective measure is to clean up and refit the window. It is important to retain historic window furniture (e.g. handles and latches) in any adaptations. In future maintenance, do be careful not to paint over the brush strips as this would clog them up and reduce their thermal efficiency.

In addition, weather-stripping can be added to other openings, e.g. doors, rooflights and skylights, to prevent heat escaping. Similarly, you could add covers over letterboxes and escutcheons (covers) for keyholes to prevent draughts. Gaps in floorboards or skirting can be draught-proofed. Where pipework pierces an external wall, such as to an undersink water pipe, it is important to ensure the opening is not creating draughts.

Draught-proofing may not be suitable in rooms producing large amounts of water vapour (such as kitchens or bathrooms) as it will reduce ventilation levels.

For spaces which are large, or encourage a through-draught, it may be beneficial to install an internal draught lobby. However, this should be reversible and discreet to avoid damaging the significance of the building.

CHIMNEY

While the chimney is not in use, a damper or a balloon can be inserted into the flue to reduce excessive heat loss (and draughts). It is also essential to ensure that there is sufficient ventilation to avoid moisture build-up and rotting of the timber bressumers (the timbers over the fireplace opening), otherwise the structure of the stack itself may become dangerous. In the winter, removing the damper or balloon and using a chimney for the purpose for which it was built – i.e. to burn wood – can be a good way of building up residual heat in the mass of the building and can help to reduce damp (although it will not be as efficient as a retrofitted wood-burning stove). Timber for burning should be sourced locally.

WINDOWS

A first step to reducing the heat loss through windows is to make sure they fit properly. After that, adding interlined curtains, internal blinds or shutters is usually the simplest course of action and often the most aesthetically pleasing and sensitive, as it involves the least intervention to the building. These options can sometimes achieve similar improvements in energy efficiency to secondary or double glazing (see below), especially once the energy used in manufacturing the glass is taken into account. They can also keep the building cool in summer, preventing heat from passing into the room in the first instance.

Where internal window shutters have become stuck shut or have been removed in the past, releasing them or putting them back should enhance the historic character of the building, as well as reducing draughts and high-time heat loss. If the original shutters are no longer available, a suitable match should be sought. To make curtains more effective, ensuring that there are pelmets above, and skirtings below, the window can help to avoid heat being lost from the room.

Where there is currently no glass in the windows, or it needs replacing, you may be able to install thermally efficient glazing to improve energy efficiency, as long as the appearance is consistent with any windows that are still in place. Low-emissivity glass reduces overheating in hot weather whilst reducing heat loss when it is cold outside. It is therefore preferable from the point of view of both the environment and comfort. However, the coating can sometimes be seen from certain angles, so it may not be appropriate for principal facades of listed buildings.

Film applied to the inside of the windows can also reduce either infra-red radiation to control heat gain or ultra-violet radiation to reduce damage to interiors and furnishings whilst allowing natural light and some heat to enter. Some films control both types of radiation and different films may be appropriate in different parts of a building, depending on the orientation of the windows and the sensitivity of the interiors. Again, the film must be selected carefully to ensure it does not alter the appearance of the windows too much.

Remember that the glass can sometimes be part of the significance of a building (e.g. historic crown glass in a Georgian crescent) and that windows can often be the most visually distinctive aspect of a building's architectural character. Changing the windows therefore requires understanding of the existing windows and careful design of the replacements. It may be more sympathetic to the character of particularly fine or sensitive buildings to use older-style blown glass, which is less reflective and has a degree of distortion. You should take opportunities to re-use glass as this meets the dual objectives of retaining historic character and making the best use of existing materials.

If the conclusion is that the existing windows and glass must remain, there is often quite a lot that can be achieved to make them fit better, thereby reducing draughts and heat loss (see the previous section on draught-proofing).

Secondary glazing

Secondary glazing is the placing of an extra sheet glass window behind the original window. It can often be appropriate and effective, reducing the U-value of the window by up to 50%.[25] It should also reduce noise. It is important to make sure that the secondary glazing is reversible, to protect the significance of the building over the long term. It should not be added where this would stop shutters from working.

Visually, the best secondary glazing systems are those which sit directly against the original window and have a compatible framing pattern – i.e. so that the secondary frame is concealed neatly behind the original. This also allows for any window seats to remain usable and traditional shutters to remain visible (and preferably usable). However, there would need to be a sufficient gap (of at least around 200mm) for noticeably reducing noise and heat loss.

When installing secondary glazing, it is important to ensure that there is still sufficient ventilation, and access for maintenance and cleaning. The window must also open wide enough to meet safety regulations in the event of fire.[26] Some secondary glazing systems can be removed easily to take advantage of passive solar gain in the summer, and reinserted for the winter to retain heat. For an example of where secondary glazing has been used effectively, please see the case study on Lauriston Place on pages 68 – 69.

Double glazing

Single-glazed windows tend to have a U-value of around 5.0U, compared with 2.9U or less for double-glazed equivalents. Although standard double glazing is usually too thick to fit into existing timber window frames without unacceptable alterations to the glazing bars and mid-rail (parts of the window frame) there are now products on the market which may make this possible. Filling the glazing with krypton rather than argon, for example, means the double glazing can be thinner (although more expensive). Meanwhile, sash and casement timber windows with few or no glazing bars can allow for acceptable installation of thicker glass. However, retrofitting double glazing can be relatively expensive.

It is important to find out how long the double-glazed units will last to ensure that they are both cost-efficient and worth the energy used in their manufacture, as well as being recyclable at the end of their lifetime. Take care, too, to ensure that the appearance is in keeping, particularly on the principal elevations. For an example of where double glazing has been installed effectively, please see the case study on Norton Park on pages 35 – 36.

Did you know: opening sash windows at both the top and bottom is best for ventilating the building; warm air escapes at the top and fresh air is drawn in at the bottom?

[25] 'Energy Heritage', p. 29.
[26] More information can be found in the Building Regulations, Approved Document B (Fire safety) – Volume 1: Dwellinghouses (2006 Edition).

HEATING, COOLING AND VENTILATION

The power required for heating and cooling a building is determined by:

- the leakiness of the building;
- the difference in temperature outside and inside;
- the efficiency of the heating system;
- the use and needs of the occupants.

Therefore you can:

- reduce the leakiness of the building (see sections on insulation and draught-stripping);
- reduce the temperature difference by turning down the thermostat;
- increase the efficiency of the heating system;
- encourage occupants to minimise their need for heating and cooling (see Chapter 8).

Timers and thermostats should be installed on hot-water cylinders and in rooms or on individual radiators, to ensure that energy for heating and cooling is only used when required. Immersion heaters are more costly and fuel-intensive and are therefore a priority for fitting with a timer and thermostat. Where sited in rooms, they should be positioned carefully, to ensure there is a free flow of air to give an accurate reading, and so that wall-mounted thermostats have minimal visual impact.

Generally speaking, it would be reasonable to set the heating to come on below temperatures of about 19°C and cooling to kick in above about 25 – 28°C.[27] 'Compensators' can be used to regulate temperatures and bring on the heating at the optimum time prior to building occupancy, according to weather conditions.

Some buildings, or parts of buildings, e.g. those used for community purposes like churches, may not need heat on a daily basis. However, it can be healthier for historic buildings to leave the heating set to 24 hours to build up a background heat but then turn down the thermostat, even as low as 15°C; this can save energy and avoid fluctuating temperatures, which can harm the building fabric.

It can be important to provide at least a low level of relatively constant background heat, especially where there are fragile items such as wall paintings, historic furnishings, textiles or works on paper. Churches are especially susceptible to damp and especially difficult to heat efficiently, but here background heat may be able to be 'topped up' by using radiant tube gas and electric heating subject to obtaining the necessary Faculties from the Diocese or relevant Denominational Committee. (A Faculty is the name for the consent granted by the ecclesiastical bodies that are granted ecclesiastical exemption from listed building consent).

[27] 'Heritage and Culture: Energy saving in historic sites and modern buildings', p. 12.

Boilers

Replacing the boiler can make an extremely important difference to the energy efficiency of a building and help you save on heating bills (using 30 – 40% less energy in some cases, with an equivalent financial saving).[28] It should be done after other attempts to reduce the thermal demand in the building, to avoid ending up with a larger boiler than is actually needed.

Hints and tips

If you are thinking of replacing your boiler, why not install a heating stem which runs on renewable energy, such as biomass, a heat pump or solar thermal panels. See the Chapter 6 on 'Moving to cleaner energy' for more information.

Condensing boilers recycle heat that would otherwise be lost. They should always be used unless there are technical reasons not to do so, such as inability to sensitively locate the balanced flue. The best condensing boilers (fuelled by gas, liquid gas petroleum or oil) have efficiency ratings over 90% (meaning that less than 10% of the energy used to generate heat is wasted). A combination boiler may be more appropriate where there is little space.

In most cases, replacing the boiler should not involve an adverse effect on the historic character of the building, but it is very important to minimise the diameter of service holes and to ensure that significant plasterwork or ceilings are not cut through. Traditional lath and plaster ceilings can be quite difficult to repair if damaged. Ensure that the boiler flue has minimal visual impact (e.g. by being positioned on a secondary elevation). Wherever possible, an existing flue should be used, assuming it is not in a prominent position, and in some cases it may be possible to place the flue inside an old chimney stack.

Ventilation

This is essential for maintaining the air quality in the building and removing moisture.[29] In older structures, ventilation tends to be most effective when it is continuous, rather than just when the building is being used. Natural ventilation m aintains the building at a constant temperature without requiring the use of energy. In some cases this can save half of the energy used in air-conditioned offices.[30]

Did you know: cooling a building requires more energy than heating it? Electrical air conditioning accounts for 4% of final electricity consumption and could rise to 6% by 2020.[31]

[28] www.energysavingadvice.co.uk/energy-saving-products/energy-saving-boilers.php
[29] Problems are likely at ventilation rates below 0.5 ach (Chris Sanders, speaking at Energy Efficiency in Traditional Buildings).
[30] 'Retrofitting Soho', p. 44.
[31] 'Heat and Energy Saving Strategy Consultation', p. 12 – 13.

In many cases, original design features of listed buildings can be used, or adapted, to channel air in order to achieve a system of natural ventilation (see page 12 for more information). In addition, it may be possible to modify the internal layout of the building to encourage natural cross ventilation. However, great care must be taken not to remove walls or alter the internal plan-form, where these are part of the special interest of the building.

High noise levels outside the building can make natural ventilation problematic, as occupants will be disturbed when windows and vents are open. Mechanical ventilation or a mixed mode system – mechanically assisted natural ventilation – may be a better option in these kinds of situations.

A solar air heating system can be installed which heats the air coming in to ventilate a building. A fan (which could be powered from a renewable source, such as solar photovoltaics) draws warm air under south-facing roof slates or tiles, which have been heated by the sun. The air is then ducted into the rooms so that less additional energy for heating is required. This can be a good way to ensure the building is well ventilated whilst maintaining comfortable temperatures, and involves minimal visual and physical impact. Although this system is not widely used, an example of successful installation is provided in the case study on page 35.

Where natural ventilation is not possible, e.g. because of the design of the building or a noisy outside environment, the most energy-efficient option is a well-designed, highly efficient mechanical ventilation system (sometimes called a 'whole house' system). Windows or vents are thermostatically controlled, meaning that they open or close according to the temperature in the room. This can be assisted through the installation of a building management system, which monitors and controls temperature and air quality (see page 39 for more information on building management systems).

In systems using mechanical ventilation, heat exchangers can be installed to ensure that heat leaving the building (for example from kitchens and bathrooms in the home) is re-used to heat cold air entering the building. In this way, the used air is not wasted but helps keep a steady internal temperature. Heat exchangers can save around 60% of the heat in the extracted air.[32] Make sure any new ducts or vents associated with mechanical ventilation and heat recovery have minimal visual impact, by designing them with as few bends and junctions as possible, and situating them on less visible elevations.

Loose-fit solutions

Where it is possible to create spaces within spaces, such as mezzanines, this can reduce the area that needs to be fully heated or cooled. (It can also make the building more viable by increasing the lettable floor area.) However, remember that the plan-form of a listed building is often significant, and not all buildings will be able to sustain such sub-division. The architectural proportions of large rooms can be spoilt by the insertion of a mezzanine, however reversible its construction may appear. The benefits of loose-fit solutions also need to be weighed against possible loss of natural light and passive solar gain, and the movement of cool air around the building.

[32] 'Sustainable Energy – Without the Hot Air', p. 297.

Norton Park, Edinburgh

CASE STUDY: Norton Park, Edinburgh

Norton Park is a beautiful, red sandstone, Category B listed building near the boundary of Edinburgh and Leith. It was built as a primary school in 1903 to the designs of the architect John Alexander Carfrae. However, by the early 1990s it had ceased to be used for that purpose. In 1995 ownership was passed to the Albion Trust, which undertook a large-scale refurbishment project, converting the building to offices. Mezzanine floors were added to increase the lettable space by 25% (to 30,000 square feet) and make the redevelopment financially viable. The building opened in 1998 and currently houses 23 voluntary organisations, with 350 staff.

The project involved reducing energy loss by adding roof and wall insulation (reducing the U-values to 0.2W/m^{2}K and 0.1W/m^{2}K, respectively). Secondary double glazing units were installed behind the original sash windows (reducing the U-value of the windows to 0.85W/m^{2}K).

New systems for heating and mechanical ventilation ensure at least one air change per hour. New condensing gas boilers were installed, with heat recovery to make use of the heat from exhaust air.

Using a solar air-heating system, some of the air coming into the building for ventilation purposes is heated by up to 20°C as it passes under the roof slates to reduce the need for heating and air conditioning.

A building management system controls temperatures and lighting in the 15 heating zones. Daylight and motion sensors further avoid wasted energy for lighting.

The appointment of a facilities manager dramatically reduced energy consumption from 249kWh/m^2/year to 150kWh/m^2/year. For every square metre that is the equivalent of switching off a 60W light bulb for 1,650 hours every year. It reduced CO_2 emissions from 80 to 50 tonnes per annum. This demonstrates the importance of ensuring that the building is performing as it should be after the works have been carried out.

Rainwater is harvested from 40% of the roof and collected in a storage tank to be used for toilet flushing.

Rainwater harvesting system at Norton Park

We are most grateful to The Albion Trust, and in particular to Margaret Cameron, for providing this case study.

Example of use of original tiling and secondary glazing at Norton Park

Throughout the redevelopment project, there was a focus on re-using products and materials and leaving in place original fabric and fixtures, including ceramic wall tiles (with extra tiles supplied by the original manufacturers), cast-iron radiators, doors, wainscoting, floorboards, stone and slates. New materials were selected which had low embodied energy and low impact on the environment; for example, sustainably sourced timber, natural-fibre carpeting, linoleum and mainly water-based paints.

A key social benefit of the project is the ease of communication and networking between the different charities in the building. It also made use of local labour, and trainees, in carrying out the works. It has helped to revitalise a run-down area, increasing employment and investment.

A Feildbarn Eco-pod, Yorkshire Dales

CASE STUDY: 'Feildbarn' Eco-pods, Yorkshire Dales

The architectural practice Feilden Clegg Bradley Studios (FCB) is leading a team to attempt to solve the problem of the dereliction of traditional field barns in the Yorkshire Dales. The landscape in this area, in common with many parts of northern England, is characterised by a large number of remotely sited stone field barns within fields bounded by stone walls. They are an important part of the landscape.

Many of the barns are no longer viable to use for agricultural purposes, but strict planning controls to conserve their character limit the scope for alteration, and many of the buildings have been falling into disuse and disrepair.

FCB has developed a model to break this vicious circle, by using an innovative loose-fit solution to convert these barns to short-term accommodation.

Conversion first involves repairing the fabric of the barn to the highest conservation standard using traditional materials and techniques for like-for-like repair. A free-standing 'eco-pod' is then inserted inside the barn to allow the building to be used without modifying the fabric itself; at the end of the project the pod can be dismantled and recycled, if and when necessary, leaving a repaired barn.

Two typical field barns in the Yorkshire Dales
© FCB Studios LLP

The pod itself is highly insulated with sheep's wool insulation, and low energy-lighting is installed to minimise energy consumption.

Services are mounted on an adapted agricultural trailer, which is towed to the barn by tractor or 4x4. The service trailer is located outside the barn, providing occupants of the pod with drinking water and hot water, which is heated by solar panels mounted on the trailer roof. The trailer also provides heat and electricity from a mini combined heat and power (CHP) facility, which uses liquid petroleum gas (LPG), but it is hoped that a local source of biogas will soon become available as an alternative fuel source. When the building is not in use, the trailer can then be removed from the site.

We are most grateful to Feilden Clegg Bradley Studios, and in particular Geoff Rich and Miriam Kelly, for providing this case study.

The Feildbarn team includes the Bolton Abbey Estate, who have provided a barn for the construction of a prototype installation, and Linford Group, who constructed the experimental eco-pod with funding from the Yorkshire Dales National Park Authority. An economic appraisal has been carried out with support from Yorkshire Forward. Over the life of the test project, which currently has planning consent for one year, the environmental performance of the eco-pod will be monitored. However, it is planned that a larger-scale test of the project, providing accommodation in a number of barns, will be implemented in 2010.

Interior of a Feildbarn Eco-pod © FCB Studios LLP

This innovative re-use project is an excellent example of the principle of adapting the conversion to suit the building – and not adapting the building to suit the pre-conceived conversion!

Building management systems

A building management system allows you to control the ventilation system, heating, cooling and lighting in different parts of the building at different times of day. For example, in offices they can be linked to the meeting room booking system so that lighting, heating and cooling are only switched on when a meeting room is going to be in use. Movement, or occupancy, sensors could be installed as part of a wider building management system, so lights come on only when people are present. Similarly, daylight sensors can control artificial lighting according to what is required in different areas of the building, based on natural light entering the building from outside. Building management systems may be most cost-effective for larger buildings, and buildings used for commercial purposes.

ORGANISING SPACE

Waste and recycling

Make sure, wherever possible, that there is sufficient space for separating and storing recycling, both inside and outside the building. Where there is a garden, try to accommodate composting facilities. The local authority should be able to advise you on what materials are collected for recycling in the area. Some offer discounted or free composters.

Sustainable travel

Similarly, find space for cycle racks where possible, to encourage users of the building to travel by bicycle.

Drying space

If the building is to be used for residential purposes, consider where clothes can be dried naturally, to avoid the need for energy-consuming tumble drying.

FIXTURES AND FITTINGS

Whether or not the building is undergoing extensive changes to the fabric, you should fit more efficient fixtures and fittings (such as lights, taps and electrical appliances), at the very least when existing ones come to the end of their life, and sometimes sooner, if the energy saved is likely to outweigh the environmental costs of replacement.

Radiators and pipework

Installing or replacing radiators with more efficient models may help to improve the energy efficiency of the heating system. However, you should consider carefully the appearance of the radiators, to ensure they are sympathetic to the character of the building. New pipework should be situated carefully to minimise visual and physical impact. Similarly, new holes in the building fabric should be minimised, e.g. by re-using existing service routes. The addition of reflective panels and radiator shelves allow the reflection of heat back into the room but should not be added if this would involve fixing to historic panelling or significant plasterwork.

Where the radiators or pipework are themselves features of special interest, they should be used as part of a modernised building, or at least kept in situ, wherever possible. If they must be removed, they should be photographed and recorded beforehand.

Plumbing

Energy and water use should at least be metered – and, where applicable, sub-metered – to allow measurement of consumption and incentivise resource efficiency. Ideally, and particularly for larger buildings, systems should be installed which monitor water use throughout the day, detect leaks and identify high use and wastage.

If showers, toilets and taps are being replaced, water-saving models should be sought to conserve water resources, including spray taps, dual flush toilets and low-flow showers. Flow restrictors can be fitted to pipework to minimise water use. If toilets are not being replaced, bags can be inserted in the cistern to reduce water used for flushing. Waterless urinals can also be cost-effective, saving up to 30% of the water used in offices.[33] Similarly, energy-and water-efficient white goods should be chosen.

The Government's Water Technology List contains products which meet specified water-saving criteria (see the 'Useful links' section at Appendix C for more information).

Hints and tips

Businesses purchasing these products qualify for enhanced capital allowances tax relief on 100% of both the cost and installation of the products.

Refurbishment of the building also offers an opportunity to simplify hot water systems that often involve unnecessarily long and unsightly piping.

You might wish to consider composting toilets, which use a number of methods to break down waste product and turn it into a valuable resource for gardening. Although composting toilets will not be suitable for many buildings, they could, for example, be worth thinking about at properties with large numbers of visitors (see pages 78 – 79 for a relevant case study).

Did you know: on average one person consumes 150 litres of water per day? Toilet flushing accounts for about 30% of domestic water consumption, and even more in offices.[34]

[33] 'Retrofitting Soho', p. 76.
[34] 'Retrofitting Soho', p. 76.

RAINWATER HARVESTING AND GREY WATER RECYCLING

Water consumption is currently estimated to be at least 150 litres per person per day, on average. The Government plans to reduce this to 120 – 130 litres by 2030.[35] At the highest level of the Code for Sustainable Homes, water consumption is 80 litres per person per day. Although this applies to new build, it sets an important standard to aspire to. Usually the only way to achieve this level is by installing a system which collects and re-uses water.

Recycled rainwater can be collected from roofs or the ground and filtered. In theory, it can be used for a variety of (non-potable) purposes, including in washing machines or for flushing toilets, car washing, irrigation of gardens and grounds or cleaning walkways or paved areas.

Rainwater harvesting fits well with Sustainable Urban Drainage Systems (SUDS) requirements to eliminate extra surface water resulting from new development on build sites: rather than simply collecting the surface water in attenuation tanks and releasing it gradually into the drainage system, the water in these tanks can be pumped back into the building to be re-used. Rainwater harvesting can typically save around 50% of a home's mains water needs and up to around 80% in an office.[36]

The design of some roofs may make them unsuitable for rainwater harvesting – for example where there are many gables it will be difficult to capture water from the several down pipes. The drainpipes themselves must have sealed, rather than open, gulleys to ensure that the water is of a sufficiently good quality.

In terms of visual impact, the system will require new pipework, which must not be allowed to damage the significance of the building. Rainwater harvesting may therefore be more appropriate as part of a bigger refurbishment where floors and/or walls are being replaced. You will need to find space (usually underground) for a storage tank. If the tank needs to be situated above-ground this may require planning permission.

The size of the rainwater harvesting tank will depend on the following factors:

- roof area;
- average rainfall;
- efficiency (i.e. how much of the water is lost in transit);
- demand for water in the building (so that water is turned around at least every 18-20 days, creating storage space for new rainfall).

Retrofitting a rainwater harvesting system can be expensive, and so are replacement filters, although not all systems require these. As a general rule, the payback is most favourable where the building has a large roof area coupled with a high demand for water.

[35] 'Future Water: The Government's Water Strategy for England', p. 22.
[36] Save the Rain: www.savetherain.info

Some late-Georgian-type buildings are characterised by low hipped roofs behind a parapet and with a central well that may be a lightwell for the staircase or is sometimes designed to collect water, which is then carried away discreetly (to avoid downpipes on the principal elevations) or stored for domestic use. Where this still exists it may be easily adapted to modern use. In other cases a specialist surveyor would need to assess that the structure is sound enough to take a new water tank. Conversion of 19th century industrial buildings also presents opportunities with large roof areas and a robust construction that can accommodate the necessary tanks. For an example of where rainwater harvesting has been used effectively, please see the case study on Norton Park on pages 35 – 36.

For homes, it tends to be more appropriate to use the collected water just for watering gardens because of the complexity of integrating the system into the building's pre-existing plumbing system. This means a relatively larger storage tank is needed, in order to store water in the winter for use during the summer. However, commercial systems can normally be retrofitted more easily. Even where these systems are not appropriate, rainwater can be collected in water butts and used for watering gardens.

'Grey water' is water which has already been used in the building – for example in baths, showers or basins. Similarly to rainwater harvesting, grey water can be re-used for toilet flushing. An advantage of grey water recycling is that the amount of water that needs to be stored is normally less, because it is coming into the system on a daily basis rather than only when it rains. This means the storage tank can be smaller. However, it is more difficult to install and maintain than rainwater harvesting.

In general, water recycling systems may not be a sensible option where space is at a premium because of the need to accommodate storage tanks. Note too that some manufacturers will not guarantee white goods where they are used in conjunction with rainwater or grey water, although there should not be technical obstacles, so you should check this beforehand. You must also make sure the rainwater or grey water cannot flow into the mains supply and contaminate it.

APPLIANCES

Electronic devices account for as much as a quarter of household electricity use in the UK; the Energy Saving Trust expects this to rise to around 45% by 2020.[37] You may find you can reduce appliance consumption by up to 30% by switching to more efficient (A or A* rated) appliances. The largest gains can often be made by choosing more efficient refrigerators, computers, printers and televisions, and ensuring they are turned off at the wall rather than left on standby.

For televisions, or museum display screens, liquid crystal display (LCD) screens use less electricity than cathode ray tube (CRT) displays and give off half as much heat, saving energy and making it easier to keep the building cool.

[37] 'The Ampere Strikes Back', p. 3.

LIGHTING

Moving to energy-saving light bulbs – either compact fluorescent lamps (CFLs) or light-emitting diodes (LEDs) – can drastically reduce carbon emissions from buildings as they use between 2 – 20W (rather than 50 – 60W used by traditional bulbs) and last up to 40,000 hours. This means you can save over two thirds of the energy used to light the building. Research by Historic Scotland showed that changing all lighting to CFLs in a cottage dating from the mid-1800s can reduce total lighting energy consumption by up to 76%.[38]

Efficient halogen lamps are also now available which, although not as efficient as CFLs or LEDs, use around half of the energy of old-fashioned light bulbs whilst maintaining the same visual appearance. Energy-saving light bulbs will also save you money: over 12 years, the amount spent on lighting can be reduced by 80% by switching from incandescent bulbs to low-energy bulbs.[39] Meanwhile, the National Trust saved 2,223 tonnes of carbon, and £430,000, per annum as a result of their 'big switch' to energy efficient light bulbs.[40]

In any case, old-fashioned light bulbs will be phased out from 2011. However, it makes sense to replace them immediately, even if they are not worn out, because of the amount of energy and money you will save.

Tubular daylight pipes or solar light pipes transfer daylight from the roof to internal spaces through 'light tubes' lined with highly reflective material. They may be particularly appropriate, for example, for lighting and ventilating toilets and bathrooms on upper floors. They can be combined with artificial lighting (for when there isn't enough daylight available). However, it is important to consider the visual impact of the tubes and pipes.

Where there are special lighting requirements, for instance for museum exhibits, not all energy saving options will be suitable – for instance, CFLs give off ultra-violet radiation. However, alternatives are quickly becoming more readily available. Triphosphor fluorescent tubes, for example, create a more natural, brighter light. Fibre-optic lighting is also extremely energy efficient and has the advantages of being both discreet and non-damaging to museum collections. Adequate ventilation is still essential and, where fans are needed to keep the light source cool, noise can be an issue.

LEDs are becoming increasingly efficient. They are already particularly appropriate for communal areas or floodlighting and it is likely that the colour rendering will be improved in the future, making them more suitable for internal use (particularly museum collections, as they have no ultra-violet rays).

Meanwhile, where low-level lighting is needed at night-time, for instance in gardens and outside spaces, you could consider installing 'solar lights' which absorb sunlight during the day and light up after dark.

38. 'Energy Modelling in Traditional Scottish Houses', p. 19.
39. 'Sustainable Energy – Without the Hot Air', p. 58.
40. Dave Burges, Natural Trust, speaking at the South East and London Historic Environment Forum Event Time and Tide, November 2008.

Denton Hall, Ilkley, Yorkshire © NG Bailey

CASE STUDY: Denton Hall, Ilkley, Yorkshire

Denton Hall is a Grade I listed mansion, set in 2,600 acres of farmland in the heart of the Yorkshire countryside. It is the head office of national building services provider, NG Bailey, having been bought by the company in 1979, and also operates as the firm's training academy.

Sustainability is at the heart of NG Bailey, both in the work it delivers for clients and across its own estate. So, in 2006, the company embarked on a schedule of work that would result in improved environmental performance of all its offices, as well as at Denton Hall – a journey that would be challenging because it is a listed, stone-built, high-ceilinged, draughty property which must retain its visual impact.

With these parameters in mind, a team of the company's own engineers set about the task, which included the following:

Installation of solar thermal panels

- With over 75% of Denton Hall's energy consumption coming from oil usage, there were significant savings to be made from using solar panels to heat the domestic hot-water supply.
- The panels required very precise positioning in relation to the sun, to maximise solar energy conversion.
- The optimum location was identified at the front of the building. They had to carefully design ground-level, natural camouflaged units to comply with listed buildings regulations.

The use of energy-efficient lighting

- With lighting contributing up to 60% of electricity consumption at the Hall, improvements were imperative.
- Denton Hall has 17 chandeliers with 344 light bulbs; specialist suppliers matched and replaced the candle-shaped bulbs with their more environmentally friendly counterparts.

Introducing the correct building controls

- 11 wireless sensors / monitoring units were installed, creating 'zones' in which energy consumption would be measured.
- An intranet-connected Tridium Intelligent Building Management system was installed throughout. This, for example, means that lights are switched on and off according to when a room is booked for use.
- A large screen in reception shows the latest consumption statistics, which in turn helps to raise awareness of the energy-reduction programme.

Solar thermal panels at Denton Hall © NG Bailey

Internal communications

One of the biggest challenges in reducing consumption was engaging the users of the Hall. The use of technology cannot improve energy consumption alone; the desire has to be embedded within the culture of an organisation, so NG Bailey set out to change the hearts and minds of its workforce through an internal communications campaign, including a screen located in reception which displays real-time energy-performance information.

The company continues to improve environmental sustainability, including through the planned installation of a biomass boiler. It is well on its way to hitting its energy-reduction target for the Hall.

We are most grateful to NG Bailey, and in particular Colin Robertson and Nicola Ayscough, for providing this case study.

BUILDING MATERIALS

Did you know: in the year 2000 the manufacture and transport of building materials accounted for 10% of UK CO_2 emissions?[41]

Eight key principles for sourcing materials:

1. Retain and re-use original materials wherever these are available, making use of the embodied energy of those materials rather than wasting it. For instance, wall and roof tiles, doors, radiators, floorboards and wainscoting can all be salvaged.

2. Source second-hand and recycled materials, for instance by insulating with recycled newspapers, plastic and glass.

3. Source materials locally. When carrying out works to a listed building, there is already an imperative to use materials sourced from the same place as those used in the original construction or, if that is impossible, to use similar available materials. This ensures that the historic character and appearance of the building is maintained or enhanced. Sourcing locally is, of course, an important part of minimising environmental footprint as well as maintaining historic integrity.

4. Choose durable materials so that less energy is wasted in the long term. For example, although imported slates may be cheaper, they tend to fail quicker and often have a different texture and colour to indigenous slates.

[41] Jane Anderson, BRE, speaking at the Government Historic Estates Unit seminar Cutting Down on Carbon, 2007

5

Select natural materials with a low embodied energy[42] which will often be most appropriate anyway. They include:

- wattle and daub
- unfired earth – clom / cob
- lime mortar
- lime wash
- straw
- hemp
- reed
- hair
- timber
- natural fibre carpeting

Lime mortar generates less CO_2 than cement-based mortars in its production and reabsorbs CO_2 as it hardens. It is breathable and allows natural movement in historic buildings, avoiding structural problems further down the line. It also allows for future adaptation of the building because stones can be re-used much more easily.

Some of these, such as hemp lime and straw bales, even absorb and store CO_2 and therefore have negative net emissions.

Other natural materials, such as slate, stone, flint and granite, have a higher embodied energy but you might still need to use them in moderation, in order to repair the building sensitively.

6

Avoid materials with high embodied energy. Cement should be avoided both for environmental reasons and for the conservation of the heritage. It traps moisture inside buildings and has a high carbon footprint, accounting for some 3% of greenhouse gases.[43] It will also be out of keeping with the historic character of a listed building and, because it is not breathable, will not be healthy for the historic fabric. Similarly, using PVC for windows creates a significant quantity of chemical waste and only has a lifespan of 20 – 30 years – while PVC windows are perceived as being maintenance free, this is not in fact the case. They can also be very difficult to recycle. On the other hand, well-made and properly maintained wooden windows can be repaired to last for hundreds of years, and re-used (or even used to generate energy by burning) at end of their life. Aluminium, steel, cast and wrought iron, lead and copper also have a relatively high embodied energy so should be used sparingly and recycled.

[42] For more information about the embodied energy of different materials, see the table on page 325 of 'Sustainable Energy Without the Hot Air'.
[43] 'Lose or Re-use', p. 18.

7 Opt for sustainably sourced wood (e.g. wood certified by the Forest Stewardship Council, FSC). Indigenous UK hardwoods tend to be expensive but are much more sustainable than imported tropical hardwoods, especially as the latter may not last as long in exposed locations. It is particularly important not to be wasteful in using softwoods, as so much energy is used in transporting them and treating them, and they cannot easily be re-used. Sweet chestnut and Douglas Fir can be good options, where they fit with the character of the building and come from sustainably managed sources, as the trees grow relatively quickly and the wood is durable. However, remember that, as a general rule, the faster the timber grows the poorer it will weather unless well-maintained with an effective paint system.

8 Use water-based paints, where possible, as they have a smaller environmental footprint than oil-based and emulsion paints. However, where oil paints are required (e.g. because the surface is wood or metal) traditional oil paints, composed of linseed oil and turpentine, are best. Timber (e.g. oak) can be oiled rather than treated to stop leaching, which is better for the environment and gives a more traditional left-to-weather appearance. Staining or coloured preservatives should be used sparingly and are often not traditional.

Hints and tips

Construction should be undertaken with consideration for the easy removal and recycling of building products at a future date.

To address the issue of waste produced during the works to the building, you should also implement a site waste management plan (this is a legal requirement for construction work costing over £300,000). More information is available from the website of the Department for Environment, Food and Rural Affairs (see the 'Useful links' section at Appendix C).

Where possible, purchase materials from suppliers with environmental management systems (EMS), i.e. ISO14000.

See the 'Useful links' section for links to more advice on selecting and sourcing environmentally sustainable materials.

CHAPTER 6: Moving to cleaner energy

You should focus on adapting the building to minimise the demand for energy and natural resources (see Chapter 5). A package of such energy-saving measures could reduce CO_2 emissions by as much as 46%.[44] Only after you have exhausted all the options for energy saving should you consider generating your own energy from renewable sources. (There are a few exceptions to this – for example where there is already a history of on-site energy generation, or where boilers are being replaced – in which case it might make sense to consider this earlier in the process).

Did you know: the power and heavy industry sector is responsible for 35% of UK greenhouse gas emissions?[45]

This chapter describes the various technologies which use natural energy sources to generate energy to use in buildings. Unless otherwise specified, the focus is on micro- or small scale generation, with only enough energy being generated to power one building or a small set of buildings.

Generating energy on-site may be particularly appropriate for buildings which are not connected to the gas network or national grid. This is more common in Scotland, for instance, than other parts of the UK (around 85% of UK buildings are grid connected, whilst the figure for Scotland is 66%).[46]

Hints and tips

UK registered businesses qualify for Enhanced Capital Allowances, giving them access to enhanced tax relief for investments in equipment that meets published energy-saving criteria.

You should assess the likely impact of the technology and the cost of the equipment and installation. Some issues to consider include:

- the significance of the building and how to ensure this is conserved;
- the energy demand of the building in use, relative to the power you expect to generate from the technology;
- the nature and extent of air leakage from the building and how this impacts on the effectiveness of the technology;

[44] 'Energy Modelling In Traditional Scottish Houses', p. 27.
[45] 'The UK Low Carbon Transition Plan', p. 9.
[46] David Cameron's presentation at Renewable Heritage, May 2009: www.changeworks.org.uk

- the position of the building (e.g. whether the roofs attract sunlight);
- the setting of the building (e.g. whether there is garden space for microgeneration measures like a biomass boiler or a ground-source heat pump);
- the size and visual or physical impact of the technology and any associated pipework;
- the nature of the local area (e.g. in a relatively dense urban area it could be more efficient to install technologies on a larger scale – for instance, community heat systems may be viable where there is a heat demand of more than 3000kW per square kilometre and sub-metering is possible);[47]
- the carbon saving over the lifetime of the building and the renewable technology itself, compared with the energy required to produce, transport and install the raw materials involved (the embodied energy). Usually there will be net positive carbon savings. However, where this is not the case, there is no environmental justification for installing the technology;
- the cost of capital, installation, feasibility and consultancy work, compared with the expected savings on energy bills;
- other studies and surveys you will need to complete, such as environmental-impact studies, archaeological assessments, and wildlife-and habitat-impact studies;
- how the building will be managed so as to maximise the benefit from the energy-saving and microgeneration measures installed (see Chapter 8).

! *Bear in mind that quoted carbon savings only relate to the particular building assessed, and the circumstances of your building will certainly be different, giving higher or lower savings.*

ROOF-MOUNTED TECHNOLOGIES

In many cases, where you propose to mount renewable technologies on the building, a feasibility study and structural survey will be essential.

There is a risk that tiles and slates may be broken during installation and later maintenance, so it is important to ensure that spares are available. Roofs with stone or handmade tiles may be expensive and difficult to replace, and drilling through them could render them unusable. In some cases, other parts of the building such as windows may be at risk of damage (e.g. as solar panels are being hoisted into position). In general, pre-fabricated systems are easier to install, as long as they are appropriate for the building.

[47] 'Heat and Energy Saving Strategy Consultation', p. 91.

If there are bats or birds in the roof you should take advice before carrying out any works affecting the roof, as all UK bats, and some birds, are protected by law.[48]

SUPPLIERS

It is advised to procure products and installation services from companies which are part of the UK Microgeneration Certification Scheme. Associations representing suppliers of individual technologies may also have their own codes of practice which apply to member organisations. The key one is the Renewable Energy Association's REAL Assurance Scheme, and for solar thermal technologies there is the Solar Keymark Certification Scheme. It is important to be aware that if you are applying for grants to carry out the work, you will often need to use specified accredited installers and products.

Using a single company, or partnership, to install all parts of the system can help to ensure the installation process runs smoothly.

It is important to get several quotes and take a realistic view on the level of energy generation made possible by your particular building and site – the output of the technology will vary in different circumstances. Asking for 'measured performance information' should give a more realistic assessment. You might be able to get a contract which includes a commitment by installers to provide ongoing technical support.

Hints and tips

Consider how maintenance will be carried out throughout the life of the equipment, and ensure that the parts are sufficiently accessible.

Make sure the installation can be removed and replaced relatively easily in the future, if necessary, as technology advances and more efficient systems become available.

It may be possible to set up a community 'hub', for example if the building is a school or community centre, whereby several buildings in the area could benefit from the energy being generated, or synergies could be realised in the supply and transportation of fuels, repair of equipment, etc.

[48]More information is available from the Bat Conservation Trust and the RSPB (see 'Useful links' section at Appendix C). A joint publication by English Heritage, The National Trust and Natural England has also been published on 'Bats in Traditional Buildings' and is available to download from the HELM website (see 'Useful Links').

HEATING AND HOT WATER

Did you know: heat accounts for 49% of all primary energy consumed in the UK? Buildings account for almost 50% of the UK's heat requirement, with a roughly equal split between commercial and residential sectors.[49] More than three-quarters of the energy we use in our homes is for heating our rooms and water, accounting for 13% of the UK's greenhouse gas emissions.[50]

Using electricity for heating produces 430g CO_2 per kWh. That's around 7 tonnes of CO_2 per year for a two-bedroom household. Gas heating is much cleaner, at around 190 – 250g CO_2 per kWh but it is still responsible for substantial CO_2 emissions. This is why renewable technologies are a much better alternative: the technologies described in this section produce CO_2 emissions close to zero. (You could also generate electricity from renewable resources and use it for heating – see the next section on 'Electricity'). They may be particularly worth thinking about if you are already planning to replace the boiler.

Legionella

Stored hot water must be heated to 60°C regularly to avoid the risk of legionella bacteria forming. Therefore, top-up systems will be needed for when this level of heat is not being generated from renewable resources (e.g. during dark hours where solar thermal panels are being used). You can connect a separate boiler to the same tank to heat the water to the required level.

It is important to remember that heat energy should be generated as close as possible to the building, as it loses efficiency when transmitted across distances.

Opposite is a decision tree which suggests the technologies you might think about first, based on your requirements. This is only intended as a rough guide to the options most likely to be available and appropriate; the detailed information in the following text contains fuller advice about the available technologies.

[49] 'Why waste heat?', p. 3, 9.
[50] 'The UK Low Carbon Transition Plan', p. 10.

Figure 5: *Heating decision tree.*

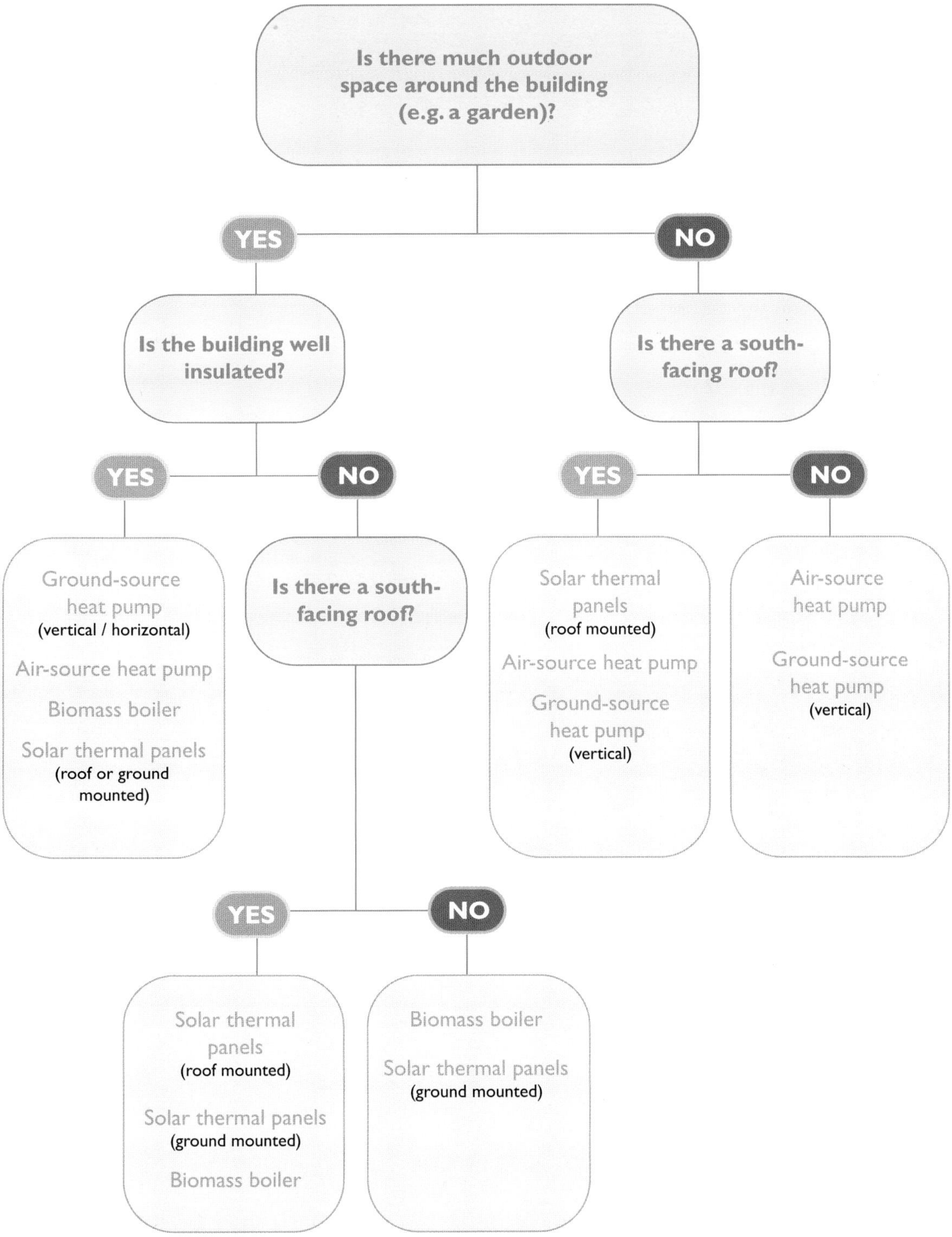

Heat pumps

Heat pumps use warmth from the air, ground or water to supply heating or hot water to a building. They can often meet all of a building's space-heating demand. Since they require electricity to run, heat pumps are not strictly 100% renewable (unless that electricity is also coming from a sustainable source). However, they only require one unit of electricity to produce up to around 4 units of heat, whereas a conventional efficient boiler will only produce about 0.8 – 0.9 units of heat from a unit of electricity.

Heat pumps perform best where the building is relatively well insulated and air-tight because they produce less heat than conventional boilers (this is less of an issue, for example, for biomass systems). They tend to produce an average water temperature of 35°C. They can provide background heat which, being on all the time, builds up a residual heat that should not require topping up except perhaps in the most used areas, such as sitting rooms or offices. Where they are used to heat water rather than space, directly, a back-up system could be important.[51]

Most often heat pumps are combined with underfloor heating because they lose efficiency when combined with a conventional radiator distribution system. Therefore they tend to be most appropriate for buildings which already have underfloor heating or can accommodate it – e.g. buildings with partly raised floors, or where existing electrical space heating is being replaced. Alternatively they can be used with over-sized, or fan-assisted, radiators. Where this is the case, remember that radiators will feel cooler to the touch than before as the heat pumps provide lower level but more stable, continuous heat. Heat pumps take some time to react to changes in temperature settings so are less appropriate where temperatures are required to fluctuate throughout the day.

Some heat pumps (most commonly air source heat pumps) can be reversed to provide air conditioning in the summer. However, this can reduce the efficiency of the system and is obviously much less desirable than relying on natural ventilation, which requires no energy input at all.

When a heat pump is first installed, it can cause a spike in electricity demand which can, in a very few instances, result in a drain on the local network. This may make the capacity associated with grid connection essential (utility companies can perform a 'load check' to ascertain the power of the local supply). Alternatively, for properties where there is likely to be insufficient supply to cope with this, a 'soft start' component can be added so the heat pump begins working more gradually.

[51] 'Renewable Heritage: Microgeneration in Traditional and Historic Homes', p. 53.

Duchy of Cornwall Estate Office, Herefordshire

CASE STUDY: Duchy of Cornwall Estate Office, Herefordshire

The Herefordshire offices of the Duchy of Cornwall were converted by the former owners of the Guys' Estate during 1999 into a farm manager's residence from traditional half-timbered farm buildings previously utilised as lambing sheds. In 2001 the decision was taken to use the buildings for the Duchy of Cornwall's Hereford district office. Initially the converted buildings were heated by an oil boiler using a conventional wet radiator system.

During 2006, as part of the Duchy of Cornwall's aim to reduce carbon emissions from its directly managed properties, various alternative energy heating systems were considered, including woodchip biomass, wood pellets and ground-source heat pumps. The decision was eventually made to replace the existing oil boiler with an IVT 11kw ground source heat pump, which was supplied by Ice Energy Ltd and installed by a local plumbing firm.

Four horizontal heat loops were installed in the adjoining field to the office, each of 200m laid some 1.2m below ground level.

The offices, which are not listed, extending to some 200 square metres, were not ideally suited to the retrofitting of such a system; however, the 11kw unit (the largest which could be installed utilising a single phase electricity supply) has coped well with inherent air movements found in this type of historic building.

The heat pump unit was installed in the kitchen at the former location of the oil boiler. The installation cost amounted to £11,000, which compared favourably with woodchip at £22,000 and wood pellets at £15,000, all costs exclusive of VAT.

From a user perspective, the heat pump is simple and clean to operate and requires very little maintenance. The pump is powered on a 100% green electricity tariff.

Ground source heat pump unit, Duchy of Cornwall Estate Office

Installation of horizontal heat loops in the adjoining fields to the Duchy of Cornwall Estate Office

During the year prior to installation, the offices consumed some 3,500 litres of heating oil. Utilising the DEFRA conversion factor for burning oil, a reduction of some 8.8 tonnes of CO_2 can be calculated, which has reduced the CO_2 output from this particular office by some 24%.

The system has performed well since the date of installation, providing more than sufficient heat and hot water for the buildings, with energy-cost savings indicating a payback period of approximately 10 years.

We are most grateful to the Duchy of Cornwall Estate, and in particular David Curtis, for providing this case study.

Air-source heat pumps

Air-source heat pumps (ASHPs) use heat from the air outside the building to heat the inside. They do this via water heating or using a fan to heat the space directly. Their performance varies with the temperature of the air outside, but as UK average temperatures are almost always above 0°C, our climate is well suited to air-source heat pumps. They can be particularly well suited to the ambient air in coastal areas.

The heat-exchanger (or external fan) itself is normally a white box approximately 1m high and will need sufficient space around it to receive a free flow of air. If it has a problematic visual impact, it may be possible to site it away from the building, for example in an outbuilding. ASHPs may work well where there are large areas of flat roof to provide adequate ventilation and space to install coils and other related equipment. Similarly, any ducting or flue associated with the ASHP (i.e. if it is running on exhaust air) would need to be added with least intervention to the historic fabric and appearance of the building. Indoors you will need to factor in sufficient space for the hot water tank or cylinder. Finally, it is worth bearing in mind that ASHPs can be relatively noisy, although some of the newer models are quieter.

Ground-source heat pumps

Ground-source heat pumps (GSHPs) use warmth from the ground (usually coming from the sun heating the ground, but sometimes partly from geothermal energy from deeper within the earth). They can provide hot water or heating and cooling for a building. In one case ground-source heat pumps were able to save a further 20% in conjunction with savings from reducing energy demand, of 46%.[52]

Ground-source heat pumps can be vertical, using deep boreholes to house the 'ground loop', i.e. the piping through which water travels to be heated. Alternatively, they can be horizontal, using a shallow trench to house a straight or coiled ('slinky') ground loop. The horizontal system requires a larger area of outdoor space for a trench: to give an indication of this, even a relatively small domestic system would need a space around the size of a tennis court. This kind of system is cheaper but less efficient than the vertical type, which performs very consistently due to the almost constant temperature of the ground below about 15m (at around 11°C). However, the necessary excavation work can be very expensive.

Although most of the UK's geology is suitable for GSHPs, they cannot be installed, for example, in sandy ground or rag stone. They may also be inappropriate where the water table is high, owing to flood risk. Understanding the geological conditions (which are very well mapped in the UK) is essential for ensuring that the correct drilling techniques are used. Bespoke tests of the thermal properties of the ground could be worthwhile for large-scale jobs and cost from around £10,000. Similarly it is important to consider the level of the water table, as drilling down for the heat pump can release jets of water.

Sizing the heat pump correctly is important: oversizing can damage the compressor, whereas undersizing will result in boosting the energy supply from other sources. They are typically sized to provide around 60% of peak heating requirement or 50% of domestic hot-water demand.

52. 'Energy Modelling in Traditional Scottish Houses', p. 27.

This requires an understanding of geographical and geological conditions and of how much heat is being lost from the building. For instance, in the north the ground can sometimes be colder, so a bigger ground loop is required, whilst a smaller loop is needed in granite than in clay. It is important to avoid extracting so much heat that freezing occurs; this requires a sufficient length of piping in the ground relative to the energy demand. As a rough guide, a relatively leaky building, used for domestic purposes, is likely to require a 14 – 16kW heat pump.

GSHPs are generally most cost-effective when used in a large building or complex of buildings, owing to the relatively large amount of energy they can produce; they can be ideal for large industrial buildings, for example. The cases studies on Castle Howard (on pages 59 – 60) and on the Duchy of Cornwall Estate Office (on pages 55 – 56) are good examples of where GSHPs have been found to be effective.

Bear in mind that drilling the trench or borehole is not always included in the price of installing the pump. It can be difficult to identify a good-quality contractor to do this work, as it does not fall within an accreditation scheme, in contrast to the supply of the main GSHP technology.

Ground-source heat pumps and air-source heat pumps

GSHPs tend to be quieter than ASHPs and last for longer as they are not exposed to the outdoors. While ASHPs could be expected to last 20 years and maybe more, GSHPs have a longer lifespan of around 40 years. Both will outlast most boilers. ASHPs are cheaper to install but are less efficient, although it seems likely that their efficiency will continue to improve in the future. The fact that GSHPs are hidden from view makes them particularly appropriate for listed buildings. However, they need space and access for drilling so are most suitable for buildings with gardens or grounds. The associated plant can also be quite considerable, and so it is only appropriate for a building that has sufficient service space to house it – ideally in an adjacent outbuilding. In an urban environment, ASHPs might be more appropriate, as long as there is somewhere discreet, yet well ventilated, to house the unit and the noise is not creating a nuisance to neighbours.

Water-source heat pumps

Heat can also be drawn from water. The technology is the same as for GSHPs, except that the pipework is underwater instead of underground. A water-source heat pump can work, for example, where there is a relatively large and deep lake (at least about 5m deep) or a spring. (Very occasionally, a river system can be introduced, but these are rare: they require, for example, relatively pure water of temperatures above 5 – 8°C, and if the water needs to be pumped up to a significant height, this limits the energy savings.) Water temperatures are more variable than those underground but, on the other hand, as water is a good conductor this can assist the efficiency of the system.[53]

[53] 'Renewable Heritage: A Guide to Microgeneration in Traditional and Historic Homes', p. 51.

CASE STUDY: Castle Howard, Yorkshire

The construction of Castle Howard began around 1699. However, the buildings, along with the surrounding lakes, temples, monuments and grand mausoleum, were not completed for about another 100 years. This spanned the lifetime of three Earls and several architects, most famously Vanburgh and Hawksmoor. The building was crowned by a dramatic masonry dome, which was the first of its kind in an English private residence.

In 1940 a calamitous fire destroyed the dome and nearly 20 rooms, as well as numerous national treasures, leaving the building open to the skies. From the 1950s the Howard family has been undertaking a gradual but extensive programme of restoration and conservation. The site is now both a private residence and a tourist destination, receiving around 200,000 visitors per year.

Castle Howard, Yorkshire: digging a trench for the connecting pipework for the ground-source heat pump

The Castle Howard Board of Directors wanted to not only reduce the running costs of the business, which had risen rapidly over the past decade, but also release funds for the conservation of the building and landscape. On the other hand, they were also keen to make a positive contribution to improving the environment.

Drained lake at Castle Howard showing positioning of coils

The old oil-fired heating system used around 85,000 litres of fuel per annum. Proposals for a biomass boiler were considered but rejected, primarily on the basis of prohibitive costs of refurbishing and enlarging the boiler room. In the meantime, alternative proposals for a heat pump were worked up. The large diameter of the existing pipework was thought to make this a viable option.

To echo the operation of a heat pump, an experiment was carried out which involved removing all the time clocks from the existing system and reducing the temperature of the existing oil boilers from 75 – 85°C to 55°C. This resulted in a reduction in fuel use of 20,000 – 30,000 litres per annum, and provided a more stable environment for works of art in the house, without compromising on the comfort of the occupants. The boilers also worked more efficiently, with fewer problems and therefore less maintenance.

The conclusion was that a heat pump would work well, and English Heritage and the local planning authority were very supportive of this innovative project.

Pipe trench for pipes running to the boiler room at Castle Howard

It was decided to install a ground-source heat pump, installing coils into the reflecting lake to the north of the main house, with pipes run at a depth of 1m from the lake to two heat exchangers in the boiler room, which were in turn connected to the existing heating system. The system currently heats the main house, and it is hoped that it might be possible to extend the system in the future to include the estate office and four residential flats in the laundry block adjacent to the main house.

In the first three months of its operation, the heat pump has delivered really positive benefits.

The cost of heating the main house has fallen to between one-tenth and two-fifths of the cost of running the previous oil-fired system, which would indicate a payback period of no more than 6 years on the capital invested in the new system. It is also estimated that the pump has resulted in a reduction in carbon output of between 50% and 75%.

An educational programme is being developed to share the learning from this project, and demonstrate that renewable technologies can work for heritage buildings. This is aimed at schools, colleges and other visitors to Castle Howard.

Heat pump units in boiler room at Castle Howard

Boiler room showing boilers and heat pump units

We are most grateful to the Castle Howard Estate, and in particular Simon Howard and Henry Rayment, for providing this case study.

Biomass

Biomass involves generating energy from organic matter: burning woody materials, such as cardboard, wood and waste pellets or straw. Where plant material is used, the carbon dioxide released is offset by the amount absorbed during the life of the plants. In one case, biomass was able to save a further 35% of CO_2 emissions in conjunction with savings from reducing energy demand, of 46%.[54]

Whilst not generally applicable, biogas (derived from breaking down organic materials) may be a sensible use of available resources in an agricultural setting. Similarly, Energy from Waste facilities can provide a sustainable heating supply, by making use of heat produced by burning waste. (Methane gas from landfill sites can also be captured and used for energy.) These latter kinds of solutions will be geographically specific of course, and will tend to operate most efficiently on a large, district-wide scale.

Biomass boilers

Biomass boilers use energy generated from biomass to heat water or space in a building. Most commonly, woodchip or wood pellets are used as fuel. Woodchip systems can be more effective (and cheaper) when used on a larger scale. A rough guide to the pros and cons of each fuel is provided in the table below. This is for indicative purposes only; actual costs should be confirmed with suppliers).

Table 1: Biomass: woodchip and pellets

Fuel	Boiler price	Fuel price	Storage	Ease of feed	Efficiency
Woodchip	More expensive	Cheaper	More space needed (around 4 times as much)	More difficult	Less efficient
Pellets	Cheaper	More expensive	Less space needed	Easier	More efficient

Unlike conventional boilers, biomass boilers are most effective when they run constantly at 100% efficiency. Therefore, when sizing the boiler you should opt for one which meets around 60-90% of the heating need and use a buffer tank at times of higher demand.

54 'Energy Modelling in Traditional Scottish Houses', p. 23.

Biomass boilers are often a good option for listed buildings, as they do not require much intervention to the historic fabric. However, they will not be suitable for all buildings. When considering whether biomass is appropriate, and where it should be housed, you should think about the following issues.

- Is there a readily and locally available supply of materials for combustion (within 30 – 50 miles)? If the building is part of a sufficiently large wooded estate, biomass could be a particularly cost-effective option.

- Is there sufficient space to house the boiler and a large hot water cylinder, and to store fuel? Sometimes there are minimum deliveries of around 1 tonne for pellets and 5 tonnes for chips. If fuel is being delivered infrequently, you will need more storage space.

- Is there sufficient access (of within 20m)[55] for the vehicle delivering fuel to get close enough to pipe the fuel into the store?

- Are the users of the building prepared to undertake the manual element associated with biomass boilers (e.g. removing pot-ash and feeding the fuel into the boiler where this is not done automatically)?

- Could the installation of a biomass system be affected by local authority restrictions relating to smoke control and air quality?

- Can the flue be positioned to avoid any negative visual impact (e.g. in an existing chimney)?

The necessary height of the flue (currently 6m) will often determine the location of the boiler, as it will be too tall and prominent on many traditional and small buildings. However, on larger buildings it might be possible to vent the boiler through an adaptation of the existing stone or brick chimney. Note that it may be necessary to line the existing chimney, which can be expensive.

The biomass boiler does not need to be situated in the building itself if this would damage the building's significance, or there is lack of space for storing or delivering fuel. The Prince's Regeneration Trust is aware of schemes where biomass boilers are successfully housed at distances of up to around 400m. If siting the boiler away from the building you would need to assess the amount of heat lost in transmission, ensuring pipes are buried deep enough, and insulated sufficiently well to retain the heat.

Using biomass to heat rooms directly (rather than via heating water) implies a more significant visual impact than if heating water, with large pipes needed to channel the air. It is also important to bear in mind that, where biomass is used for hot water, a 'back-up' hot water system is likely to be needed when there is not enough demand to make it worthwhile to use the boiler (e.g. in the summer).

[55]'Renewable Heritage: Microgeneration in Traditional and Historic Homes', p. 40.

Biomass and heat pumps
Biomass boilers may be more suitable than heat pumps for buildings that are not so well insulated. They also make it easier to control temperatures. However, they can take up more space and sometimes require more care and maintenance from occupants.

Biomass stoves (which usually burn wood) are smaller in scale and less efficient than boilers but can be more suitable for smaller domestic purposes. However, they still require a sufficiently large internal space or living room becaue of the large amount of heat they produce.

Hints and tips

If you are using your own biomass fuel, don't forget to factor in the lead-in time for the fuel to dry out.

When negotiating contracts for fuel supplies, you might want to make sure you have a guaranteed supply and fixed price for a set number of years.

An example of a Swedish thermal-mass log burning boiler used for space heating at Gibson Mill

An example of a biomass boiler at Gibson Mill

Llanerchaeron is an 18th century Welsh gentry estate, encompassing a country house by John Nash, a working organic farm, two restored walled gardens and extensive parkland. It is owned and managed by the National Trust.

Gilfach goch, an outlying farmstead, was renovated between 2006 and 2008 for use as long-term volunteer accommodation, a workshop and a toilet block. Although Gilfach goch is not listed, the buildings are of historical interest.

A district network was then installed to provide hot water and space heating to the buildings. The network uses energy from a combination of 25kW wood pellet biomass boiler, and ground-mounted solar thermal panels.

In addition to the work on the outbuildings, work was carried out on Pontbrenmydyr (pictured opposite), a Grade II* listed recently refurbished clom (cob) thatch cottage, used as a holiday let. A 10kW wood pellet biomass boiler, including ground-mounted solar thermal, was installed to provide space and water heating. This was considered to be the best option because heat pumps would have been very difficult to retrofit or too expensive, whilst the cottage was too far from other buildings to be part of the district network.

The biomass boilers require minimal maintenance, with the removal of ash no more than twice a year, vacuuming of the burner after every 500 hours of use, and an annual service. They are expected to reduce CO_2 emissions by over 90%.

Biomass boiler system on the Llanerchaeron Estate

In all cases, insulation was added to the loft to reduce energy demand (mainly sheep's wool but with Tri Iso 9 where space was tight). A heavy curtain was added over the front door. It is estimated that heat loss has been reduced by at least 30%.

Throughout the renovation work, existing materials were re-used wherever possible. Water-based paints, estate wood, A-rated appliances and rainwater harvesting systems were used to minimise the environmental footprint of the work.

Pontbrenmydyr after refurbishment

Pontbrenmydyr before refurbishment

We are most grateful to the National Trust, and in particular Keith Jones, for supplying this case study.

Pontbrenmydyr before refurbishment

Pontbrenmydyr after refurbishment

Solar thermal collectors

Solar thermal collectors capture and store the sun's heat via water-storage systems. They are powered by daylight so can work even when there is cloud cover as well as in direct sunlight. The energy is normally used for supplying hot water to the building, at temperatures up to 60°C, which can be stored for limited periods of time in well-insulated water tanks. They are therefore most appropriate for buildings which are in frequent (often domestic) use, with sufficient hot-water demand. Solar collectors can technically be used for heating the building, and may increasingly do so in the future, but this would require much more roof area.

> **Did you know:** *in a typical UK location the average raw power of sunshine per square metre of south-facing roof is about 110W/m² and the average raw power of sunshine per square metre of flat ground is roughly 100W/m²?*

Since the availability of solar heat tends to coincide with the need for cooling, solar thermal panels can also be ideal for linking to cooling (rather than heating) systems. However, fuelling the cooling system requires water of a higher temperature. Special collectors can produce temperatures up to 250°C, which may also be useful for buildings housing industrial processes.

Solar thermal technology is unlikely to be able to provide all of the building's space or water-heating demand but could be used to supplement the main system (be it a heat pump, biomass or non-renewable technology).

Evacuated-tube solar collectors are the most efficient, transferring around 40% of energy collected from the sun to the heated water; flat plate collectors transfer about 30%.[56] This means that evacuated tubes require less surface area on the roof. However, they also tend to be more expensive, more fragile and more conspicuous, so can have a damaging impact on the appearance of the building.

Collectors should be positioned at a 30° angle to the sunlight for optimal performance but can still be effective at a shallower angle, especially in summer when the sun is higher. They operate most efficiently on at least around 4m² of south-east to south-west roof receiving direct sunlight during the main part of the day, so may not be appropriate for smaller buildings. They can still work on east-or west-facing roofs but will produce a lower annual yield. The individual collectors do not need to be located together as a block but can be positioned separately.

The solar collectors can be fitted on top of the roof or can be flush fitted to replace the roof surface. The former method is more appropriate for listed buildings, since it is relatively reversible. (Flush fitting often looks better but might involve irreversible damage to historic roof timbers.) The collectors normally protrude by about 125mm set into aluminium frames, although they are increasingly low-profile. They should not be mounted on principal roof slopes but may well be installed on roofs which cannot be seen from the ground, such as shallow roof pitches on tall urban buildings, roofs partly hidden behind parapets or the roof slopes to central valleys.

[56] www.solar-trade.org.uk

Different designs of panels are available in a wide range of appearances, so find those with the most complementary appearance. Mounting the panels themselves only involves piercing the existing roof for the pipework, but the latter involves the removal of the existing roof cladding and fixing to the actual roof structure. Where the roof covering needs to be replaced anyway, this provides an excellent opportunity to install solar panels. However, it is important to consider, at the design stage, what will happen when the technology eventually becomes obsolete and needs removing or replacing.

Solar collectors should not be fixed to a thatched roof, as a flat and stable surface is required on which to mount them. If the roof is flat, collectors can be mounted horizontally, or on a tilted frame. In the case of felt roofs, the felt should be replaced at the same time as collectors are installed. Lead roofs present some challenges in terms of contraction and expansion of the lead over time and the way that cables and fixings are applied; the solar collectors would need to be fixed in the top third of the lead roof.

As an alternative to mounting the collectors on the building itself, they could be mounted away from the building: for example if they would have a detrimental visual impact or the requisite sunlight conditions are lacking (see the case study on pages 44 – 45.) However, excavation required to bury the pipes may not be appropriate where the site is archaeologically sensitive. The pipes would need to be well insulated so as to minimise the heat lost in transmission. However, remember that even if a small amount of the heat is lost before it reaches the building, the energy is coming from a renewable source so there is still an overall carbon saving.

It is essential with this technology to have space to house a relatively large hot-water cylinder with a capacity of at least around 120 litres (about 0.5m in diameter and 1m tall) and maybe in excess of 200 – 300 litres (1.5 to over 2m tall) for larger buildings. Larger, taller cylinders tend to be more effective, as the water at the bottom of the tank is cooler.[57] This could replace the existing hot-water cylinder or could be additional to it. As a rule of thumb, about 35 extra litres of space is needed for every extra square metre of collector on the roof.

Solar thermal energy may be unsuitable for buildings which have little space and would require significant alterations to the fabric to accommodate a larger tank. Additional pipework will also be needed, and must be factored in alongside the installation of the panels themselves.

Hints and tips

If a single cylinder is installed, check that it is compatible with your boiler, as solar thermal systems cannot be used with all combi boilers.

You could think about incorporating solar photovoltaic cells (see below) to power the pump circulating water around the system, reducing its environmental footprint still further.

[57] 'Renewable Heritage: Microgeneration in Traditional and Historic Homes', p. 34.

Lauriston Place © Changeworks

CASE STUDY: Lauriston Place, Edinburgh

Changeworks, an Edinburgh-based environmental organisation, has worked with social housing provider Lister Housing Co-operative on two demonstration projects improving the environmental sustainability of Georgian (1820s) Grade 'B' listed tenement flats in central Edinburgh. The buildings lie within the Old Town Conservation Area and form part of a UNESCO World Heritage Site.

Energy heritage

In 2007/8 the partnership carried out a range of sensitive measures to reduce energy demand in nine flats within one tenement stair. These measures included:

- secondary glazing (a bespoke product designed for historic buildings);
- draught-proofing;
- shutter refurbishment;
- new 'A'-rated condensing boilers;
- floor insulation (a new and innovative slimline system suited to historic buildings);
- top-up loft insulation;
- low-energy lighting;

- smart monitors (to allow householders to see their energy use in real time);
- home energy advice visits.

The annual energy consumption of each flat was reduced by an average of 5,000kWh (and in some cases up to 12,000kWh). This equated to CO_2 emission reductions of an average of over 1 tonne per year, and in some cases up to 2.4 tonnes. (The application of all measures would reduce CO_2 emissions by 36%.) Meanwhile, annual energy costs fell by an average of £175 (and in some cases up to £400).

Renewable heritage

In 2008/9 solar water-heating systems were installed to meet around 50% of the annual hot-water needs of tenants in 49 flats in seven stairs of the buildings. To minimise visual impact the solar thermal panels were 'hidden' in the inner valleys of the Georgian M-shaped pitched roofs. This allowed the panels to be sited discreetly without compromising their efficiency, as the roof ridge runs from east to west and the panels face south. The total cost of the work was just over £4,000 per flat.

The partnership plans to provide a further two stairs of flats with solar heating systems, with solar panels mounted on angled frames on top of flat roofs. The visibility of these panels will also be negligible, owing to the height and situation of the buildings.

Changeworks has published two comprehensive guides on energy efficiency and microgeneration in traditional and historic homes (see the 'Useful links' at Appendix C and Bibliography at Appendix E).

Installation of solar thermal panels at Lauriston Place. Reproduced courtesy of Edinburgh World Heritage

Secondary glazing at Lauriston Place © Changeworks

Solar thermal panels on roof at Lauriston Place © Changeworks

We are most grateful to Changeworks, and in particular Nicholas Heath, for providing this case study.

ELECTRICITY

At the moment most of our electricity comes from centralised power stations, which often run on fossil fuels. One problem with this is that much of the energy is wasted before it reaches customers. Most power stations also have a significant carbon footprint: gas-fired power stations typically produce 385g of CO_2 per kWh, while those using coal account for around 755g per kWh. (Nuclear is associated with lower carbon emissions of up to 11 – 22g per kWh.)[58] There is therefore a clear case for generating more electricity from renewable sources. This section considers the different micro and small-scale technologies available.

Storing excess electricity

Peaks and troughs in energy generation do not always match well with patterns of demand. One way to manage this is to export excess energy back to the national grid and, by doing so, earning revenue from energy suppliers. To do this, you would need to connect your electricity generation system to the grid, which requires permission from the Distribution Network Operator (DNO). You can find details of your DNO from the Energy Networks website (see 'Useful links' at Appendix C). Make sure you contact them well in advance of starting to generate electricity. In addition, revenue can be generated through the sale of Renewables Obligation Certificates and Levy Exemption Certificates. If feed-in tariffs become available, you will find it easier to sell back electricity being generated on a small scale. See Appendix A on Funding and finance for more information.

Where grid connection is not feasible (e.g. because the building is not mains-connected in the first place) you could store excess electricity in batteries. Batteries do, however, require a significant amount of storage space, and other special requirements, including relatively cool temperatures and plenty of ventilation.

When selecting a type of battery, some issues to consider are:

- capacity/energy density: how much energy is stored per kilogram of battery storage;
- efficiency: how much energy you get back per unit of energy put in;
- lifetime (this is usually around 10 years);[59]
- cost.

Lithium-ion batteries tend to store the most energy (110 – 160Wh/kg compared to 45 – 80 for nickel-cadmium) and are 88% efficient, whilst nickel cadmium-batteries last the longest (1500 cycles of energy storage, compared with 300 – 500 for lithium-ion). Nickel Metal Hydride (NiMH) batteries also perform fairly well on each of the above criteria.[60] Research is ongoing to develop batteries which can store more energy in the future.

[58] 'Why Waste Heat?', p. 9.
[59] 'Renewable Heritage: Microgeneration in Traditional and Historic Homes', p. 63.
[60] 'Sustainable Energy – Without the Hot Air', p. 199.

Hints and tips

You should be able to site electricity-generating technologies further away from the building than those producing heat and hot water, because less energy is lost in transmission. This can sometimes help to avoid damaging the appearance and fabric of more sensitive buildings.

Electricity can also, of course, be converted into heat for heating spaces or water. This may be an increasingly efficient option in the future, when more of our electricity comes from renewable sources.

On page 73 is a decision tree which suggests the technologies you might think about first, based on your requirements. This is only intended as a rough guide to the options most likely to be available and appropriate; the detailed information in the text below contains fuller advice about the available technologies.

Solar photovoltaics

Solar photovoltaics (PVs) convert energy from daylight into electricity, using a semi-conductor material such as silicon. There are a number of PV technologies, including (in order of both efficiency and life span) polycrystalline, monocrystalline and amorphous silicon (thin-film). If the system is more efficient the array of PVs need not be so large. Hybrid systems are also available which combine more than one of these technologies in several layers. However, amorphous silicon can be preferable for listed buildings, as it is lighter and can be mounted on curved surfaces. It is also sometimes more effective than the other types in cloudy conditions.

To generate most energy, the array of cells needs to be mounted on a south-east-to-south-west facing roof, receiving direct sunlight during the main part of the day. Alternatively, you can mount them on east or west faces, but the amount of energy produced will be lower. The cells will not be effective on north faces. Mounting the cells at a 30° angle gives the best performance, but this can be reduced to a flatter angle (down to about 15°) if necessary. In the same way as for solar thermal panels, flatter angles will give a greater yield in the summer and steeper ones in the winter.

For the cells to work efficiently you will need to make sure they are:

- not shaded (e.g. by trees or other buildings), as this will stop them from working;
- kept clean from dirt;
- sufficiently ventilated.

Solar PVs can be mounted either as raised panels in aluminium frames or they can be flush fitted (sometimes in the form of tiles). The former only involves piercing the existing roof for the cables but the latter involves the removal of the existing roof cladding and fixing to the actual roof structure. Flush fitting looks better but might involve irreversible damage to historic roof timbers.

It is also more expensive. Therefore the former approach will usually be more appropriate for listed buildings, as it can be reversed. However, if the roof needs replacing anyway, then integrated cells could be considered (see the case study on pages 85 – 88).

Again, it would not be appropriate to mount the cells on the main elevations owing to the detrimental visual impact of this. Nor would it be suitable to attach PVs to thatched roofs. For flat roofs, the cells can be fixed to a tilted frame or mounted horizontally. Listed buildings with flat roofs, the surface of which is not visible from the ground, may be particularly suitable for PV installations. Just as for solar thermal collectors, if the roof is made of felt or lead, you should replace this at same time. If the felt already needs replacing, this could be a good opportunity to install solar PV. If the roof is made of lead, the PV cells should be mounted on the fixed section, at the top third of the lead sheet. It is important to be aware of the potential for expansion and contraction when siting fixings and cabling.

PVs are not appropriate for some roofs: for example, those covered in stone tiles or slates laid in diminishing courses, where the regular shape of the PVs would conflict with the varying coursing of the traditional slates. The flatness of the cells would also conflict with the wavy appearance of clay pantiles.

The arrays come in many colours, shapes and sizes so you can choose ones which suit the appearance of the building. They are highly reflective and so make a definite change from the traditional matt surfaces of slate, stone or clay tile. It is therefore very important on significant buildings to select the least conspicuous arrays or mount them on the adjacent ground (usually on a frame or a mast). This will require excavation for foundations and cabling, which may or may not be permissible, depending on the archaeological sensitivity of the site.

Costs of PV are falling, but it is still an expensive technology, particularly when retrofitting rather than integrating into a new build project. However, it can be a viable solution.

In terms of the net carbon cost, a roof-mounted, grid-connected solar system can generate around four times the amount of energy consumed in its manufacture over a lifetime of 20 years.[61]

Solar PV and solar thermal panels

Installing solar PV costs around four times as much as solar thermal and only produces about half as much energy, although this is electrical energy rather than heat. Combined systems also exist, which deliver both energy and hot water by pumping water past the back of the photovoltaic units, where it is heated. This could reduce the intervention needed to the roof, because only PVs and not solar thermal collectors are needed, in return for the same amount of energy.

[61] 'Sustainable Energy – Without the Hot Air', p. 41.

Figure 6: *Electricity decision tree.*

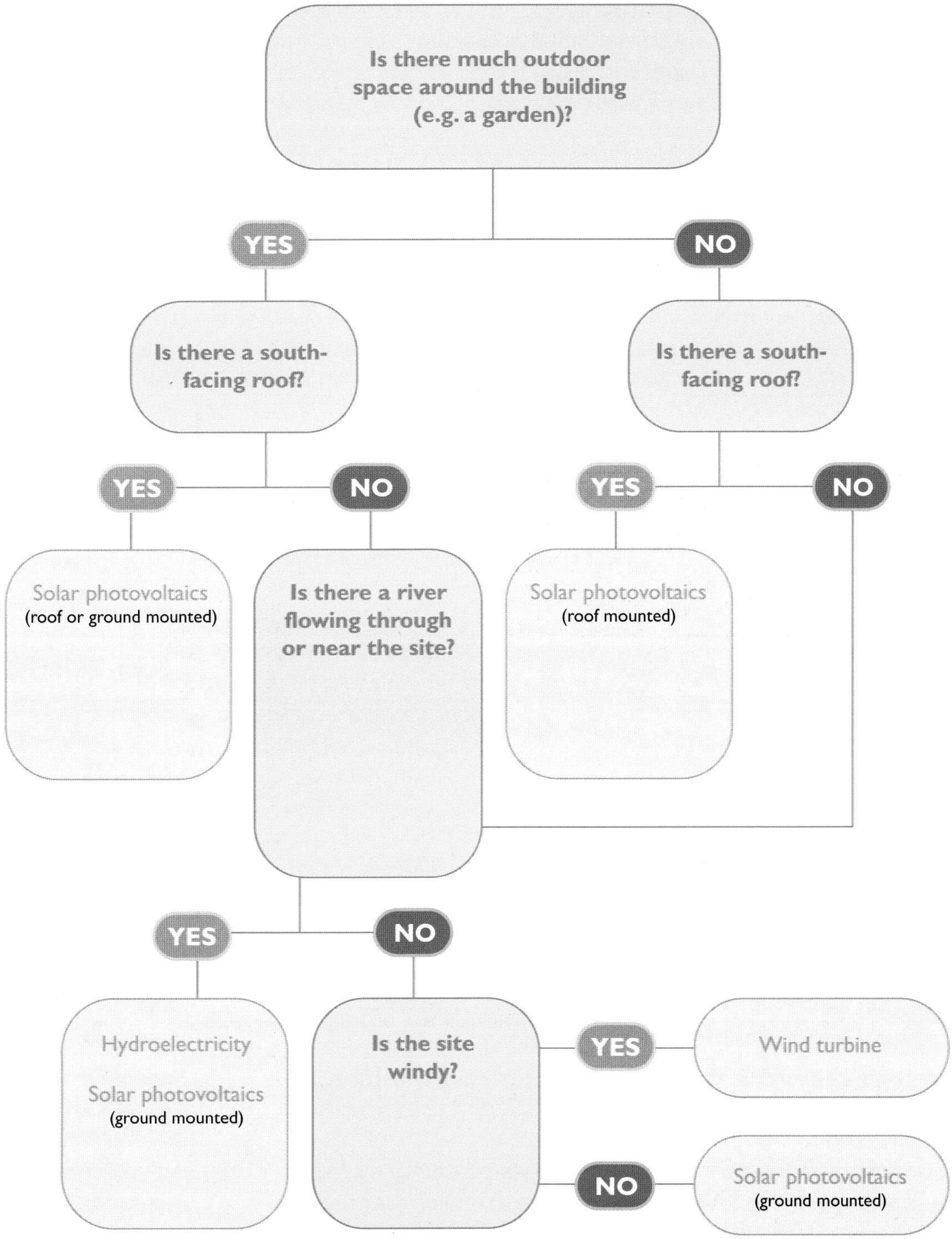

CASE STUDY: St James's Church, Piccadilly, London

St James's Church is a Grade I listed parish church in London's West End. It was designed by the office of Sir Christopher Wren and consecrated in 1684. It probably illustrates Wren's vision for the internal layout of a town parish church better than any other, with galleries to allow all the members of a large congregation to hear the preacher.

The church was hit during the air attacks of the 'Big Blitz' winter of 1940 – 41, leaving it ruined and roofless for nearly seven years until post-war repairs began. In more recent times, a further major restoration project has begun to bring it back into good condition.

As part of this work, two rows of photovoltaic panels were installed on the south-facing roof to generate electricity from sunlight, for lighting and appliances in the building. A grant for £16,000 was provided by EDF Energy's Green Energy Fund, with remaining project costs met by the Energy Saving Trust and the church itself.

In total, there are 40 photovoltaic panels with a rated capacity of 5kWPeak. The system runs at 0.8 – 3kW, depending on the time of year. It supplies around 3350kWh of electricity per year and currently saves around £250 per year on electricity bills. A display panel situated in the porch shows how much electricity has been generated. The energy and financial savings are relatively modest as the scheme is quite small, installed as a 'test-bed' and educational tool as much as a major power generator. St James's Church is an excellent exemplar, showing that microrenewables can be installed sensitively in such a highly listed building.

The panels are invisible from the ground, as they are screened from view by the parapet on the south roof, so there is no significant visual impact. In addition, each panel is supported by a specially designed moulded plastic box, weighed down by ballast. This means the panels just sit on the roof and there are no securing bolts or fixings holding them to it. This ensures minimal intervention to the historic fabric and reversibility when the panels eventually need replacing. They can also be moved aside very easily when the roof is subsequently renovated. The black cable bringing the power down from the roof has also been sited sensitively.

Rows of solar photovoltaic panels on the roof of St James's Church

Securing the panels using ballast

St James's Church, Piccadilly, London

We are most grateful to Finna Ayres of St James's Church, and Simon Dawson, for providing this case study.

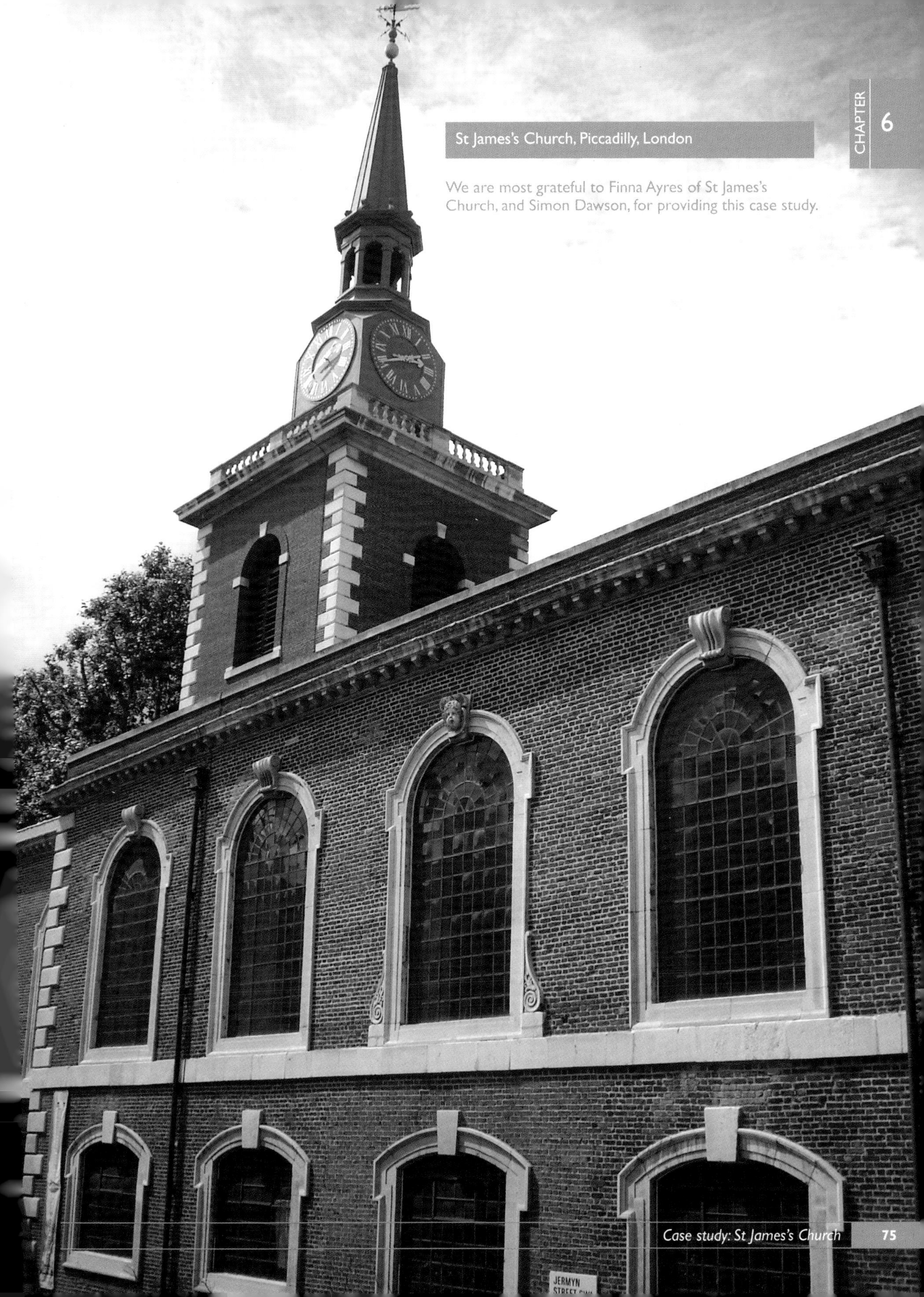

Wind

Wind turbines convert the energy from the wind to electricity. Machines of 1kW are normally used for individual buildings. They can be free-standing or mounted on the roof.

The turbine needs to be positioned where it has a clear, smooth and steady fetch to the prevailing wind (normally south-west). This can be prejudiced by obstacles like trees, buildings and other tall landscape features. If the wind speed is below 4.5m per second, a wind turbine is very unlikely to be financially viable, since the amount of energy produced would not justify the capital cost; the Energy Saving Trust suggests only considering a turbine where the local annual average wind speed is at least 6m per second. It is relatively rare to have access to this kind of wind speed near to a building in most parts of the UK. Wind speed prediction tools are available online, including from the Energy Saving Trust's website.

For roof-mounted systems to be effective, turbines generally need to be at least 0.5m above the roofline, and often higher, where the wind is stronger and more consistent. However, it will rarely be appropriate to mount a wind turbine on a listed building because of the visual impact and structural concerns when in operation. Timber-framed structures will almost always be unsuitable.

In the relatively unusual event that a building-mounted wind turbine is suitable, the minimum number of fixing holes should be made, and should be made into the mortar joints, in order to minimise intervention to the fabric of the building. Turbines should not be attached to chimneys as this can cause damage. If the building is timber-framed, the fixing must be to the frame itself, rather than to infill panels.

Where space is available, it is usually better to mount wind turbines away from the building. This requires proper foundations and buried cable, and therefore excavation, which may or may not be possible depending on the archaeological sensitivity of the site. Although wind turbines are now usually relatively quiet, there may be restrictions relating to the distance from neighbouring properties. It is important to consider the impact of a turbine on local wildlife, e.g. birds and bats. You will also need to think about the visual impact on the landscape, particularly in or near to specially designated areas, such as Areas of Outstanding Natural Beauty and National Parks.

There are a small number of historic windmills around the UK, and they provide an excellent opportunity to harness wind power in a listed building, preserving or even enhancing their historic significance in the process.

Hydroelectricity

Hydroelectric power comes from turbines placed within a flow of water, driving a generator that converts that energy into electricity.

The amount of energy produced depends on the speed of the water flow and the vertical distance (the head) through which the water falls. A higher head will also make the system cheaper to install as smaller turbines and less equipment will be required. Because of seasonal variations, a back-up power supply is required. However, an advantage of hydroelectricity is that it can be generated fairly constantly and predictably, in comparison with technologies which rely on wind or sunlight. Moreover, water flow tends to be greater in winter, which is often when energy demand is higher too.

If more than 20m^3 of water is being abstracted per day, you will need to acquire a Water Abstraction Licence from the relevant environment protection agency (the Environment Agency in England and Wales, Scottish Environment Protection Agency in Scotland and the Northern Ireland Environment Agency in Northern Ireland). This is because the water is diverted from the river, channelled past the turbine and then flows back into the river further downstream. In landscape terms this has the potential to significantly affect the appearance of a river or waterfall. It is also essential to consider river conservation issues such as retaining or creating salmon passes.

Historic mill buildings originally powered by water turbines offer the ideal opportunity for installing this technology; see the example of Gibson Mill overleaf. It can also be particularly effective in hilly areas or where there are already weirs. Archimedean Screw systems, for example, can be installed alongside dams or weirs and can be very efficient. When adapting the building for hydroelectric generation make sure you do not compromise existing historic mill machinery; for example, stones and hoppers should be kept in situ and not removed to make space for new machinery and related plant.

Hydroelectric installations can be hidden below the water level, but the plant requires a significant amount of space. When part of the turbine is housed inside a building and open to the air (rather than being fully underwater) it is important to avoid water from the river flooding the plant. If the plant cannot be fitted into the existing building you will need a separate structure for the turbines. Therefore it is crucial to evaluate the physical impact of a hydroelectric installation before making any commitment. You might, for example, consider burying the penstock (which controls the water flow to the turbine).

Hydroelectric turbines can last for well over 20 years, only requiring minimal maintenance (such as changing the gearbox oil every few years and regular greasing). When sizing the turbine, make sure it can operate at maximum capacity for as much of the time as possible, as this will be more efficient.

Gibson Mill, Hardcastle Crags, West Yorkshire

CASE STUDY: Gibson Mill, Hardcastle Crags, West Yorkshire

Gibson Mill is a Grade II listed former cotton mill built in 1800 as one of the first generation mills of the Industrial Revolution. By the 1890s it was no longer needed for producing cotton cloth and was then used by the local population as a venue for entertainment until the beginning of WWII. After the war it fell out of use until the National Trust undertook an ambitious restoration project in 2005, with funding support from the Heritage Lottery Fund and the Regional Development Agency. The mill is now a visitor attraction and community centre.

The original hydroelectric turbine, which dates from 1927, was restored and has a minimum capacity of 9kW. It is supplemented by a new, smaller turbine which has a capacity of 1.5kW and operates at low river flow rates.

As part of the project, overall demand for energy and water has been reduced, for example by adding natural insulation to walls, floors and the roof, installing energy-and water-efficient appliances and developing an innovative human-operated, counter balance lift. The drinking water supply comes from a spring close to the building; there is no mains supply.

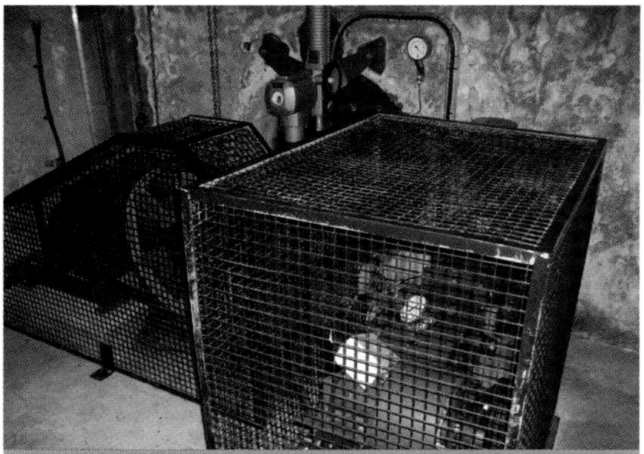

Hydroelectric turbine at Gibson Mill

Other renewable technologies were integrated into the design, with solar photovoltaics adding 3.5 – 4kW of electricity to that produced by the water turbines. Excess electricity is stored in batteries. Solar thermal panels help to meet the hot water needs of the kitchen and warden's accommodation. The visual impact of the solar thermal and solar PV panels has been minimised by locating them to resemble the type of rooflighting typical of mill buildings. Because standard fixings would have caused unacceptable damage to the roof (nearly 130 penetrations), a special mounting system was devised which was far less physically invasive, although it is visually more prominent.

A log-burning biomass boiler, with a maximum capacity of 60kW, supplements the hot water generated by the solar thermal panels (this is needed to ensure the water for dish-washing is above 60°C to meet legionella requirements). A large, 2,500 litre hot-water tank keeps water hot for long periods of time, only dropping 15 – 20°C overnight. Meanwhile, a smaller wood-burning stove provides space heating in the main room. The biomass installations use the surrounding woodland as a sustainable source of fuel.

A ground-source heat pump was investigated for this building but was not installed because the geological conditions were not appropriate.

The mill had never been connected to the national grid or mains supply gas and water. Because of this, renewable technologies were the most cost-effective option for supplying the building with heat, hot water and electricity. The total cost of the equipment and installation of the renewable technologies was £157,000, and £240,000 for all of the environmental measures (including those to reduce energy demand).

Measuring electricity usage at Gibson Mill

Recycled and traditional materials (such as clay and lime mortar) were used throughout the project. Meanwhile, a composting toilet converts waste product into a useful resource for cultivating the surrounding landscape. Sustainability is also encouraged by incentivising visitors to walk, cycle or use public transport to reach the site. As well as the considerable energy savings associated with this project, normal water usage has been reduced by up to 70%.

We are most grateful to the National Trust, and in particular Guy Laurie, for providing this case study.

ELECTRICITY AND HEATING

The technologies in this subsection can be used directly for electricity, heating or hot-water provision.

Combined (Cooling) Heat and Power

Combined Heat and Power (CHP) plants capture waste heat produced during power generation and use it to heat buildings. On larger scales it is usually associated with gas or coal plants, but smaller systems could also be powered, for example, by biomass. The heat is stored as hot water but can be used for central heating. It can also be used with an absorption chiller to convert the heat to cooling for air conditioning (e.g. in buildings used for offices). Systems which provide cooling as well as heating are known as Combined Cooling, Heat and Power plants.

The technology typically achieves a 35% reduction in primary energy usage compared with a power station and heat-only solution, with 1kW of electrical power creating around 2kW of usable heat energy.[62] However, it is worth bearing in mind that capturing the heat from electrical power generation does reduce the efficiency with which power is generated. CHP plants may also lack flexibility to deal with spikes in electricity demand and may be relatively ineffective in delivering excess power to the grid.[63] They may be more suitable than other renewable technologies where very high temperatures are required – for instance, for industrial purposes.

At the moment, CHP tends to be most efficient and cost-effective when operated on a district-wide scale, where it can run continuously. To be effective, the plant needs to be located close to a sufficient number of end users and have a high enough load factor (average power divided by peak power). The technology also works best in the context of mixed-use, relatively dense developments, where there is a balanced demand for energy and heating at different times of day and different seasons. Clearly, sub-metering would be important to establish the amount of heating and cooling energy being used by individual buildings and occupiers. Successful CHP plants operating in Woking and Southampton, for example, provide energy to institutional, residential and commercial consumers. When sizing a CHP plant, the focus should be on the heat demand of the building (rather than the electricity demand). Otherwise, more heat will be produced than the building needs, leading to waste. This does mean that the electricity supply will need topping up – either from the grid or, better still, from a renewable source.

CHP can also be used on a micro scale, for a single building, replacing the existing boiler. A unit occupying 2m^2 can currently produce 17kW of electricity and 24kW of heat[64] but systems as small as 5kW are available in the UK.

The Carbon Trust has found that micro-CHP systems can save 15 – 20% in carbon in small commercial buildings when installed as the lead boiler.[65] In some cases, though, a very efficient gas boiler may be almost as good – at least at current technologies and efficiency rates.

62 'Retrofitting Soho', p. 65.
63 'Sustainable Energy – Without the Hot Air', p. 150.
64 'Retrofitting Soho', p. 68.
65 'Retrofitting Soho', p. 69.

However, CHP may well become more viable on this scale in the future if, for example, solid-oxide fuel-cell and internal combustion engine systems emerge at a commercial level with improved electrical efficiencies.[66] In that eventuality, households and small businesses may be able to house small CHP units and export excess power to the grid.

CHP technologies may be more appropriate for very large, older buildings with high heat demands, particularly where there is already a pre-existing district heating scheme. Such buildings also tend to have the separate space needed to house the plant and large buildings, especially former industrial buildings, which might be able to accommodate a large chimney without it looking out of character. Where there is already a CHP facility nearby, it may be possible to link the building to it and make use of the energy and heat being generated.

An example of a Combined Cooling Heat and Power System, powering the Natural History Museum

[66] 'Energy Modelling in Traditional Scottish Houses', p. 2.

CASE STUDY: Natural History Museum and Victoria and Albert Museum, South Kensington, London

In 1857 the Victoria and Albert Museum (then the South Kensington Museum) opened to the public. It introduced a new style of architecture, combining influences from older buildings with modern materials and production techniques.

The Natural History Museum opened in 1881 and houses a vast collection of mineralogy and natural history exhibits. The primary building is the Waterhouse Building, by the architect Alfred Waterhouse, which is a world-famous London landmark and a striking example of Romanesque Revival architecture.

Victoria and Albert Museum, South Kensington
©Victoria and Albert Museum

Combined Cooling Heat and Power System, powering the Natural History Museum and the Victoria and Albert Museum

Natural History Museum, South Kensington, London © Natural History Museum

Both buildings are Grade I listed and are important symbols of Prince Albert's vision to provide the population with access to cultural institutions.

Until the year 2000, the buildings were part of a district heating scheme that also included the adjacent Science Museum and Imperial College. However, when those institutions withdrew from the scheme, there was a need to find a more cost-effective solution. Since that time, and with the realisation that shared services can deliver, a partnership was formed, comprising the Natural History Museum, Victoria and Albert Museum, The Co-operative Bank and Vital Energi Ltd, to install a Combined Cooling, Heat and Power (CCHP) system.

The system was completed and commissioned in December 2006. It generates 1.8MW of electricity and 1.7MW of heat at full load, powered by natural gas. This provides the majority of space heating, which operates using radiators. Absorption chillers provide 705kW of cooling. Whilst it cost around £15m to install, the system now saves over 2840 tonnes of CO_2 and £750,000 per year.

We are most grateful to the Natural History Museum and Cynergin, in particular Declan Rajasingam and Nick Ray, for providing this case study.

Geothermal

Geothermal energy comes from heat stored in the earth (from the original formation of the planet). It is usually used to provide electricity but can also supply heat directly. It tends to be used on a community-wide basis: for example in Southampton, where an 8MW CHP plant makes use of water coming straight from the ground at temperatures of around 74°C. That system saves over 12,000 tonnes of carbon emissions per year. However, because of the very specific geological conditions required for geothermal energy, which only pertain in a few parts of the UK, this solution will only rarely be appropriate. It also involves drilling down several kilometres, and so the capital outlay is extremely large.

COMBINING RENEWABLE TECHNOLOGIES

It may make sense, environmentally and economically, to install more than one type of renewable technology. For example, two or more heating technologies could be connected to a single boiler. Renewable technologies may be particularly complementary where one works well in the winter and the other in summer, e.g. biomass and solar thermal energy. However, you will need to make sure the cumulative impact does not affect the significance of the building (even though individually their impact may be acceptable).

There is currently fairly limited research and advice on how to combine the different technologies successfully, but this is likely to be forthcoming as the sector expands.

GREEN ENERGY SUPPLIERS

In some cases, generating energy from renewable sources may not be possible, e.g. because of the historic and protected nature of the building or site, or prohibitive costs. In any event, it is likely that the energy supply will still need to be 'topped up' from mainstream supply, to meet the total annual demand. You should consider purchasing energy from suppliers which generate the energy purely, or mainly, from renewable sources (offering what is often referred to as 'green tariffs') and operate with credible green policies. If your organisation currently pays the Climate Change Levy (a tax on energy bills), switching to electricity from qualifying renewable sources can exempt you from paying the Levy.

For websites where you can compare the environmental credentials of different energy suppliers, see the 'Useful links' section at Appendix C.

Did you know: if you use energy mainly during the evenings and weekends, you could save money by opting for off-peak tariffs? Ask your energy supplier for more information.

The Power House at Royal Gunpowder Mill, after the refurbishment

CASE STUDY: The Power House at Royal Gunpowder Mill, Waltham Abbey, Essex

The Power House at Royal Gunpowder Mill, before the refurbishment

The history of the Gunpowder Mill dates back to the 14th century when it was set up by the monks of Waltham Abbey as a fulling mill for cloth production. Following gunpowder supply shortages during the second Dutch War (1665 – 1667) it was converted to gunpowder production.

In 1787 the Crown took over the Mills, due to security concerns, beginning a 204-year ownership. Gunpowder was produced there for both military and civilian purposes (e.g. quarrying, construction and mining), playing a vital role in supplying explosives in WWI and the beginning of WWII.

In 1943 activities were moved to a safer location but the Mills reopened in 1945 for use as a secret explosives research centre producing rocket propellants and motors. The research centre finally closed in 1991, with part of the site converted to a museum and a resource centre in 2001.

The Power House, Water Tower and ancillary buildings were built between 1908 and 1915. This followed a terrible explosion in 1902, which killed 3 men and damaged several of the buildings; the new buildings were designed to spread out the operations across the site. Although not all listed themselves, these buildings are located within a Site of Special Scientific Interest and a Conservation Area, and are in the curtilage of a listed building (so are 'curtilage listed').

By the 1980s the Power House, which comprises a separate boiler room and engine house, was in a state of considerable disrepair. The site was bought by the Hill Group in 2007. The Power House has been sensitively refurbished and converted to provide 18,000 square feet of office space for the company's headquarters. A linked extension to the Water Tower and the refurbishment and extension of the Grade II Listed Lodge Building provides another 20,000 square feet of office accommodation. The works were completed in July 2009.

The substantial work needed to the fabric of the building provided many opportunities for making major adaptations. The environmental footprint of the building has been a central consideration of the project.

First, to reduce energy consumption, thick layers of insulation were installed in the roof, to the insides of the walls and under the floor (alongside the new underfloor heating system).

The building is naturally ventilated: windows are the primary source of fresh, cool air, using a stack effect to circulate it up through the different floors of the building. They are opened and closed automatically, in response to rainfall and changing air temperature and quality in the building, as monitored by sensors.

Interior showing natural ventilation system

Refurbished roof, clerestory lighting and roof lights

All windows are double glazed and, along with the roof lights, have been replaced using steel components, to match those originally installed in 1915.

Motion and daylight sensors control the lighting, leaving four lights on around an individual and a lit passage to the exits, even when the rest of the building is unoccupied. Meanwhile, to conserve water resources, water-efficient taps and toilets have been installed, along with two highly efficient condensing boilers.

Approximately 20% of the electricity will be sourced from a cocktail of microrenewable installations comprising:

- a gas-turbine combined heat and power plant located in the adjoining new build development, which is also linked to the underfloor heating system, to provide around 15% of the annual space heating needs and around 4% of the electricity requirements;

- 65m^2 of solar photovoltaic array (with capacity of 1kW, providing around 8% of electricity demand);

- A stand-alone, mast-mounted wind turbine located to the south-east of the building (providing 8% of the electricity – subject to final consent).

Combined Heat and Power plant for the Power House

Integration of solar photovoltaics into the roof of the Power House

Solar thermal panels mounted on frames on part of the flat roof of the new build development at Gunpowder Mill

Because the building was dilapidated, the roof had to be replaced, and this provided the opportunity to integrate photovoltaics into the roof itself. Special cells were sourced which have the appearance of historic slates, and they have been installed discreetly on two of the less visible south-facing elevations so as to be virtually invisible from the ground. A ground source heat pump was considered unsuitable in this case because the expense of drilling to a depth of 200m made it unviable.

On part of the flat roof of the new build development (the Water Tower extension), 7m^2 of solar thermal panels are mounted on frames. They are linked to a 300 litre water cylinder providing up to 60% of the building's hot-water needs.

The building's demand for hot water is relatively low for its size, as it is used for offices rather than residential purposes.

The rest of the roof is covered with sedum to form a green roof, which absorbs carbon and encourages biodiversity: the site remains a habitat for various wildlife.

The building has received a 'B' rating for energy performance, which is very good outcome for this kind of refurbishment project.

We are most grateful to the Hill Group, and in particular Andy Hill and Emma Fletcher, for providing this case study.

CHAPTER 7: Adapting to the impacts of climate change

As well as reducing greenhouse gas emissions from your listed building, the process of refurbishment or restoration offers the opportunity to ensure it can withstand the likely future impacts of a changing climate. Scientists expect that whatever mitigating action is taken now, climate change over the next few decades is already unavoidable.

For the UK, it is believed that this will mean:

- hotter, dryer summers, especially in the south of England;
- warmer, wetter winters;
- sea level rise;
- more extreme weather (e.g. storms and heavy downpours, leading to higher risk of flooding).

For buildings, this could increase the need for cooling in the summer but reduce demand for heating in the winter.

The fabric and structure of the building will be at greater risk from factors such as:

- overheating in summer;
- flooding;
- rainwater penetration;
- subsidence;
- increased weathering of porous building materials;
- insufficient capacity of the traditional rainwater goods which are not able to deal with heavy rain;
- increased condensation;
- the spread of pests, diseases, moulds, insects, fungi and invasive species;
- higher relative humidity in the winter, and lower in the summer.

To help the building deal with larger volumes of rain at once, the diameter of gutters, downpipes and hoppers can in many cases be increased to give them greater capacity to carry water away from the building. Plastic guttering should be avoided, as it is generally inappropriate for listed buildings. Due to its much shorter lifetime and difficulties with recycling the material, it can also be less environmentally sustainable than alternatives like cast iron.

Lighter, more reflective, roof surfaces can help to keep buildings cooler in summer. However, such radical change to a traditional roof should only be considered in exceptional circumstances. There are more sympathetic measures that can be taken, such as effective roof insulation. Similarly, shading and internal shutters for south-facing windows can prevent excessive solar gain as well as limiting light damage to fragile historic contents. Again, though, it is crucial to ensure sufficient ventilation to avoid condensation and decay.

Flood risk should be carefully assessed and managed to minimise the risk of damage to the building from flooding, for example by ensuring adequate drainage from the site. Similarly, the risk of structural damage from the elements should be managed through thorough and regular checks, maintenance and repairs.

With hotter, dryer summers making water shortages increasingly likely, it is becoming even more important to conserve water resources. Therefore, systems which re-use water may be even more important (see section above on rainwater harvesting and grey water recycling).

GREEN ROOFS

Areas of flat or gently sloping roof surfaces can be adapted as green roofs (e.g. using sedum). This can absorb a small amount of carbon from the atmosphere and decrease the rate at which rainwater runs off, helping to combat flood risk. Green roofs also increase the thermal mass and insulation of the roof, keeping indoor temperatures more constant and moderate as the temperature fluctuates outside. They can also encourage biodiversity. (See pages 85 – 88 for a relevant case study.) You will need to be careful to avoid damp when installing a green roof. Green roofs can also help to reduce the 'heat sink' effect of cities where in summer they become several degrees warmer than the surrounding countryside due to solar gain. This reduces overall cooling loads.

Green roofs and rainwater harvesting

Although green roofs can be combined with rainwater harvesting systems, they will tend to make those systems less effective, as the water is retained and absorbed by the green roof rather than collected and stored for re-use. However, where there is a lot of rainfall compared to the need for water in the building, a combined system could be considered.

Alternatively, where there are no flat roofs, or a green roof would be damaging to the building, balconies and gardens can also provide space for growing plants, to absorb carbon and rainfall and attract wildlife.

CHAPTER 8: Reducing demand for energy and resources – the building in use

The works to the building are only one part of the story of improving environmental sustainability. Once the building is in use, the behaviour of those who use it – either as a home, workspace or community facility – and its day-to-day upkeep, is at least as important.

Make sure users of the building understand how to operate the different technologies and systems for saving and generating energy. You may find that it is better to avoid giving the users of the building the option to override the energy controls and instead, for example, allow them simply to boost the system when demand is higher.

You would also do well to put in place environmental policies, plans and targets, and appoint a Facilities Manager who can monitor and understand the energy and water performance of the building as a whole, leading action to reduce consumption.

You can encourage building occupants to, for example:

- shut doors and shutters and draw curtains and blinds;
- turn off lights, computers and other equipment when not in use;
- minimise the use of resources like water, paper and stationery;
- reduce, re-use and recycle waste;
- travel to and from the building by foot, bicycle or public transport wherever possible;
- procure goods which have a small carbon footprint and using suppliers which operate to high environmental standards;
- wear warm clothes in winter and cool clothes in summer!
- turn down the thermostat at least to 19°C in winter (and better still, lower, only turning it up when needed);
- turn on air conditioning only when the temperature exceeds about 25 – 28°C.

> ***Did you know:*** turning the thermostat down by 1 degree can save households up to 10% on their energy bills?

There is already a great deal of information and advice available on energy-saving behaviours (see the 'Useful links' section at Appendix C).

Install 'smart meters', which provide detailed information about how much energy is being used in different parts of the building throughout the day. All homes in Great Britain will receive smart meters by 2020.

Technology is also becoming available which will allow householders to identify which individual appliances are consuming energy on a minute-by-minute basis. Analysing this data will allow you to reduce energy use still further, for example by identifying when lighting is not required and can be turned off, or encouraging different occupancy and behavioural patterns. Where there are a number of tenants in the building, it is important to ensure that sub-metering is possible for individual tenants.

Carrying out routine repair and maintenance on the building is absolutely crucial for getting the full benefit of environmentally sustainable measures. For example, make sure you seal cracks to prevent air leakage and draughts and check that windows fit properly. A full management plan should be drawn up for the building. More advice on managing and maintaining historic buildings can be found in: The Society for the Protection of Ancient Building's *Good Maintenance Guide*; their publication, *A Stitch In Time* produced jointly with The Institute of Historic Building Conservation; and The Heritage Lottery Fund's guidance on *Conservation Management Planning and Management and Maintenance Planning*. Maintenance of any microrenewable installations is also very important – suppliers often recommend annual checks.

As well as testing the performance of the building during and immediately after the work is carried out, you should reassess the building within about five years to test whether you are achieving the expected improvements, and identify any problems that have arisen since the work was carried out. This could be done using similar techniques to those described in the 'Data gathering' subsection in Chapter 4.

It is generally not possible to use a building without producing some carbon emissions. Where they cannot be avoided, you might think about a programme for offsetting carbon, for example through tree-planting schemes. Offsetting should not be seen as a solution or alternative to minimising carbon emissions in the first place but, if done through reputable organisations, supporting environmental projects is a sensible and constructive course of action.

Hints and tips

It can be healthier for historic buildings to leave the heating set to 24 hours to build up a background heat but then turn down the thermostat, even as low as 15°C; this can save energy and avoid fluctuating temperatures which can harm the building fabric. This approach works particularly well with systems using underfloor heating and heat pumps.

If the building is a tourist destination, you could consider joining a green tourism scheme, such as the Green Tourism Business Scheme (see the 'Useful links' section at Appendix C for more information).

CHAPTER 9: Summary

The reason it is so important to improve the environmental sustainability of listed buildings is not just because of their contribution to greenhouse gas emissions and, therefore, climate change, which may be relatively small. It is to equip them for a future in which energy performance and environmental credential increasingly drive decisions about whether, and how, occupiers will use a building. It is not inconceivable for these factors to be linked to the market price and taxability of buildings in the future. Therefore, The Prince's Regeneration Trust, which strives for the continued use of important heritage buildings, believes that adapting them to manage climate change is key to achieving this goal.

We hope, and believe, that this guide provides a starting point for adapting listed buildings in ways which achieve genuine environmental improvements without jeopardising what makes them important – culturally, architecturally, socially and economically.

In summary, you should always:

- **understand** the significance, design and future use of the building, and what opportunities and limitations they imply for improving its environmental performance;
- **assess** the net financial and carbon savings of each alteration, before, during and after the works;
- **reduce** the consumption of energy and water in the building before (or, in a few cases, at the same time as) considering more complicated and expensive renewable technologies;
- **generate** energy for heating and powering the building from renewable sources;
- **conserve** the building by minimising the impact of alterations on the appearance and fabric of the building;
- **share** the results of your work so others can learn from your experience;
- **maintain** the building well to make it productive and valued into the future.

It is essential that those who manage listed buildings continue to take forward this important agenda in the coming months and years. The Prince's Regeneration Trust is committed to promoting awareness and solutions, through our project, policy and educational work, and we look forward to working with like-minded organisations to make sure our important buildings of the past remain at the forefront of a sustainable future.

APPENDIX A: Funding and Finance

Alterations to save energy or generate it from renewable sources should save you money because you won't need to buy so much from energy suppliers. However, in some cases you will need to spend a relatively large amount of money up-front, and the payback period could be several months or years, depending on the technology. Therefore, it is important to consider how you will finance the up-front costs.

The Government is piloting schemes in which householders pay back installers over a prolonged period of time. In the meantime, other options are available. A reduced rate of VAT at 5% is available for energy-saving measures and microgeneration technologies. Alterations of listed dwellings may already be exempt from VAT where listed building consent is approved.

In many cases further support is available in the form of grants, loans, tax reliefs or special financing arrangements. It may also be possible to install energy-efficiency measures through initiatives such as the Carbon Emissions Reduction Target (CERT) and Community Energy Saving Programme (CESP) – see Chapter 3 and Appendix B. You might start by contacting your local authority or Regional Development Agency, or your nearest energy advice centre.

Energy service companies

One way to finance environmentally sustainable alterations, especially for large-scale, expensive projects, is through an energy service company (ESCO, or ESCo). An ESCO is a vehicle set up to lever in funding so that costs are smoothed out over a period of years, rather than being payable up-front.

The ESCO carries out the analysis and design work for the property, and installs and maintains the environmental measures. It then receives a proportion of the savings from lower energy costs, which effectively pay back the up-front capital cost (and can also be used to fund upgrades to the technology). Where no savings are made, the ESCO often bears the burden of the capital cost.

Relatively large organisations (normally in the public or private sectors) may decide to set up an ESCO themselves, partnering with energy experts; alternatively, you could contract a pre-existing ESCO. They may, however, be less appropriate for smaller organisations and buildings.

Guidance on ESCOs is available from the link below:
www.london.gov.uk

Incentives for generating renewable energy

If you are producing your own electricity you may well be able to generate revenue from this, in addition to reducing your own energy bills. First, for each megawatt hour of renewable electricity you generate, you will be eligible to receive Renewables Obligation Certificates (ROCs). To receive ROCs you need to register with Ofgem. You can then sell the ROCs to electricity suppliers, who need them to meet their statutory obligations. More information on ROCs is available from the Department of Energy and Climate Change (see the 'Useful links' section at Appendix C).

Producers of electricity from renewable sources may also be entitled to receive Levy Exemption Certificates (LECs). They are issued by Ofgem for each megawatt hour of electricity generated. To receive LECs you will need to apply to Ofgem for accredited status. Once you have received an LEC you can then sell it to an electricity supplier (which will in turn sell it to a business, enabling that business to claim an exemption from paying the Climate Change Levy). More information on LECs is available from Ofgem's website (see the 'Useful links' section).

If feed-in tariffs become available, small-scale generators of electricity will be eligible to receive a fixed price for generating and exporting electricity to the grid. Moreover, if the Government introduces the Renewable Heat Incentive, this will offer financial incentives for the generation of heat energy from renewable sources in Great Britain.

Table 2: Funding databases

WEBLINK	DETAILS
www.companygiving.org.uk	General database of funding from companies (accessed by paid subscription).
www.energysavingtrust.org.uk	Database of grants and loans for home energy-efficiency measures.
www.fundingcentral.org.uk	General funding database (free of charge).
www.governmentfunding.org.uk	General database of Government funding (accessed by paid subscription).
www.greengrantsmachine.co.uk	Database of funding for businesses to improve their environmental sustainability.
www.trustfunding.org.uk	General database of trust funding (accessed by paid subscription).

Some specific grants, loans and tax reliefs available at the time of writing are listed in Table 3 below.

Table 3: Grants, loans and tax reliefs

SCHEME	ELIGIBILITY	CLOSES	DETAILS
Big Lottery Fund	Projects in the UK	Various	Various funding programmes available for projects that bring real improvements to communities and to the lives of people most in need. www.biglotteryfund.org.uk
Bio-energy Capital Grants Scheme	Businesses, organisations and charities in the industrial, commercial and community sectors in England	2011	England and Scotland: loans for small or medium-sized enterprises of £5,000-£200,000 for energy-saving projects. Northern Ireland and Wales: loans for all businesses of £5,000-£200,000 for energy-saving projects. In Northern Ireland some businesses may be eligible for larger loans of up to £400,000. www.decc.gov.uk
Carbon Emission Reduction Target (CERT)	Householders in England	March 2011 (third phase)	Subsidies available from energy suppliers for energy-efficiency measures like loft and cavity-wall insulation, high-efficiency lighting, heating systems, appliances and energy-saving devices. www.carbontrust.co.uk
Carbon Trust loans	Businesses in the UK	Ongoing	England and Scotland: loans for small or medium-sized enterprises of £5,000-£200,000 for energy-saving projects. Northern Ireland and Wales: loans for all businesses of £5,000-£200,000 for energy-saving projects. In Northern Ireland some businesses may be eligible for larger loans of up to £400,000. www.carbontrust.co.uk
Central Energy Efficiency Fund (Northern Ireland)	Public sector bodies in Northern Ireland	Ongoing (annual)	Grants available for measures which save energy and CO_2 that cannot be financed from within existing budgets. www.dfpni.gov.uk
Central Energy Efficiency Grant (Scotland)	Public sector organisations in Scotland	Ongoing	Loans for implementing energy-efficiency measures that will reduce carbon emissions. www.energy-efficiency.org
Charity Bank	UK Charities, social enterprises and voluntary groups	Ongoing	Affordable loans for various purposes. www.charitybank.org

SCHEME	ELIGIBILITY	CLOSES	DETAILS
Climate Change Agreements	Businesses in energy-intensive industries in the UK	2013 (but may be extended to 2017)	Climate Change Agreements allow eligible businesses to claim up to an 80% discount from the Climate Change Levy. www.decc.gov.uk
Community Energy Scotland (CARES)	Community (i.e. non profit) organisations in Scotland	Ongoing	Technical grants available (e.g. for feasibility studies and development of proposals) of up to £10,000. Capital grants available of up to £150,000 towards the installation of a variety of renewable technologies. www.communityenergyscotland.org.uk/cares.asp
Community Sustainable Energy Programme (CSEP)	Community-based organisations in England	Ongoing	Project development grants available for studies investigating the feasibility of installing specified microgeneration technologies. The maximum grant available is £5,000 or 75% of the study cost (whichever is lower). Capital grants available for the purchase and installation of specified microgeneration technologies and energy-efficiency measures of up to £50,000 or 50% of the project cost (whichever is lower). www.communitysustainable.org.uk
Energy Assistance Package	Vulnerable householders in Scotland	Ongoing (awarded annually)	Stages 3 and 4 of the Energy Assistance Package provide funding for insulation and enhanced energy-efficiency measures for qualifying vulnerable households. www.scotland.gov.uk
Energy Efficiency Design Awards	Projects in Scotland	Ongoing	Awards available for up to £250,000 per project, for projects which significantly improve the energy efficiency of Scottish homes. www.energysavingtrust.org.uk/scotland
Energy Saving Scotland home renewables grant scheme	Householders in Scotland	Ongoing	Grants available for up to 30% of the installed cost of a renewable measure, up to a maximum of £4,000. www.energysavingtrust.org.uk/scotland
Energy Saving Scotland – small business loans	Small and medium-sized enterprises, private sector landlords, non-profit organisations and charities in Scotland	Ongoing	Interest-free loans for measures that reduce energy consumption or renewable energy technology installations. www.energysavingtrust.org.uk/scotland

SCHEME	ELIGIBILITY	CLOSES	DETAILS
Enhanced Capital Allowances (ECA)	Businesses in the UK	Various, depending on scheme	ECAs enable a business to claim 100% first-year capital allowances on their spending on qualifying plant and machinery. The relevant ECA schemes are: • energy-saving plant and machinery including some renewable technologies); • water conservation plant and machinery. www.eca.gov.uk
Heat Project	Homeowners, residential landlords and private tenants in Britain	Various	Grants available for loft and cavity-wall insulation. www.heatproject.co.uk
Heritage Lottery Fund	Projects in the UK	Ongoing	Various grants available for projects involving local, regional and national heritage. www.hlf.org.uk
Home Energy Efficiency Scheme	Householders in Wales	Ongoing	A package of heating and insulation improvements up to the value of £3,600. www.heeswales.co.uk
Landlords Energy Saving Allowance	Landlords of residential premises in the UK	April 2011	Landlords may claim up to £1,500 per building to install cavity-wall insulation, loft insulation, draught-proofing or insulation for hot-water systems in buildings let for residential purposes. www.hmrc.gov.uk
Low Carbon Buildings Programme – Phase 1	Householders in the UK	April 2011	Grants available of up to £2,500 per property towards the cost of installing approved microgeneration products. www.lowcarbonbuildings.org.uk
Low Carbon Buildings Programme – Phase 2	Community groups, public sector organisations and non-profit sector organisations in the UK	April 2011 *(projects must be ompleted before this date)*	Grants available for up to 50% of the cost of installing approved microgeneration products, up to a maximum of £200,000. www.lowcarbonbuildingsphase2.org.uk
NIE Renewable Grants	Projects in Northern Ireland	Various	Various grants available to businesses, householders, public sector organisations or community groups to support installation of renewable technologies. www.nie-yourenergy.co.uk

SCHEME	ELIGIBILITY	CLOSES	DETAILS
Rural Development Plan for Wales	Projects in rural areas of Wales	2013	Grants available for projects relating to one of the following four axes: Axis 1: improving the competitiveness of the agricultural and forestry sectors; Axis 2: improving the environment and the countryside; ts available for projects relating to one of the following four axes: Axis 3: improving the quality of life in rural areas and encouraging diversification of the rural economy; and Axis 4: building local capacity for employment and diversification. www.wales.gov.uk www.dardni.gov.uk www.scotland.gov.uk www.englandsrdas.com Axes 1 and 3 are likely to be the most appropriate for heritage projects
Rural Development Programme – Northern Ireland	Projects in rural areas of Northern Ireland	2013	
Rural Development Programme – Scotland	Projects in rural areas of Scotland	2013	
Rural Development Programme for England (RDPE)	Projects in rural areas of England	2013	
Salix Finance	Public sector organisations in the UK	Ongoing	Interest-free loans available to improve energy efficiency, attain targets, reduce energy bills and raise green credentials. www.salixfinance.co.uk
Scottish Power Energy People Trust	Non-profit organisations in Scotland	Ongoing	Grants of up to £100,000 for projects including making energy-efficiency improvements, with priority given to projects aimed at helping families with children and young people. www.energypeopletrust.co.uk
Scottish Power Green Energy Trust	Local community groups, not for profit organisations and charities in the UK	Ongoing	Grants available of up to 50% of the cost of installing renewable technology, up to a maximum of £25,000. www.scottishpowergreentrust.co.uk
Triodos Bank	Businesses and charities	Ongoing	Loans to support positive social, environmental and cultural change. www.triodos.co.uk
Ulster Community Investment Trust	Community organisations and social enterprises in Northern Ireland	Ongoing	Affordable loans for various purposes. www.ucitltd.com
Unity Trust Bank	Social enterprises, charities and trade unions in the UK	Ongoing	Affordable loans for various purposes. www.unity.uk.com

SCHEME	ELIGIBILITY	CLOSES	DETAILS
Wood Energy Business Scheme 2	Small businesses and social enterprises in Wales	2013	A £17m capital grant scheme which will offer grant support for wood-fuel heating schemes, small-scale electricity generation using wood and wood-fuel supply businesses. www.forestry.gov.uk
Warm Front	Householders in England	2011	A package of energy improvements up to the value of £3,500 (or £6,000 if oil central heating or a new low-carbon technology is recommended). www.warmfront.co.uk
Warm Homes Schemes	Householders in Northern Ireland	Ongoing	Insulation measures up to the value of £850 and heating and insulation measures up to the value of £4,300. www.warm-homes.com

Cost-effectiveness

Table 4 below provides an indication of the cost-effectiveness of different environmental measures. It looks at the financial payback, i.e. how long it takes to recoup the initial financial outlay through savings on utility bills; and environmental impact, i.e. how effective the measure is in addressing climate change (e.g. by saving carbon emissions).

The analysis is based on data available at the time of writing, extrapolated from several case studies and existing research. Costs and carbon savings will, of course, differ for each individual building, according to its location, size, energy demand, heat loss, remoteness, etc.

Payback estimates depend on the type of fuel the building currently uses for energy. They are likely to change as the technologies become cheaper, whilst fossil fuels become scarcer and more expensive (increasing 'brown' energy prices) and policy and regulation continues to develop.

This cost-effectiveness analysis does not take into account design and installation issues, which can also determine whether or not a technology is suitable. These are covered in the main body of the text.

Table 4: Cost-effectiveness analysis

Key:

Financial payback	Environmental impact
£ £ £ (short payback – a few months or years)	! ! ! (greater environmental impact)
£ £	! !
£ (long payback – decades)	! (smaller environmental impact)

Reducing demand for energy and resources	Financial payback	Environmental impact
Building management system	£££	!! / !!!
Double glazing	££	!! / !!!
Draught-proofing	£££	!! / !!!
Energy-efficient lights	£££	!!!
Insulation (flat roof)	££	!! / !!!
Insulation (loft)	£££	!! / !!!
Insulation (floor)	££	!!!
Insulation (wall)	££	!!!
Natural ventilation	£££	!!!
Rainwater harvesting / grey water recycling	£	!!
Replacement boiler	£££	!!
Secondary glazing	££	!! / !!!
Shutters	£££	!! / !!!
Moving to cleaner energy		
Air-source heat pump	££	!!
Biomass boiler	££	!!!
Combined heat and power	££	!!!
Green roof	££	!!
Ground-source heat pump	££	!!
Hydroelectricity	££	!!
Solar photovoltaics	£	!!
Solar thermal	£ / ££	!!
Wind power	£	!

APPENDIX B: Environment and climate change statutory requirements

Table 5: Whole UK

TOOL / MEASURE	DESCRIPTION
European Union (EU) Target	Target to limit temperature rises to 2°C above pre-industrial levels.
EU Target	Target to increase to 15% the proportion of the UK's energy coming from renewable sources by 2020.
EU Emissions Trading Scheme	Trading scheme which caps CO_2 emissions from energy intensive installations, such as combustion plants, oil refineries and factories.
Carbon Reduction Commitment (from April 2010)	Trading scheme which caps CO_2 emissions from large non-energy-intensive organisations. It aims to save at least four million tonnes of CO_2 per year by 2020.
Climate Change Levy	Environmental tax adding about 15% to UK businesses' energy bills (but does not apply where the energy comes from microrenewables). Organisations which pay the Levy can receive a discount of up to 80% through 'Climate Change Agreements', whereby they agree and meet challenging targets to improve energy efficiency or reduce greenhouse gas emissions. They can also obtain Levy Exemption Certificates if they purchase electricity from qualifying renewable sources. Target to get 40% of the UK's electricity from low carbon sources by 2020 (with around 30% from renewables).
Low Carbon Electricity Target	Requirement for electricity suppliers to source an annually increasing percentage of electricity from renewable sources.
Renewables Obligation	A Renewables Obligation Certificate (ROC) is issued for each megawatt hour of renewable electricity generated. Anyone producing renewable electricity can register with Ofgem to receive ROCs. Generators receive these certificates for the renewable energy they produce, which are then sold onto suppliers for the latter to meet their obligation. (The money paid as a penalty by those not meeting the obligation is distributed among those who did, creating an incentive to meet the obligation rather than paying the buy-out price.)
Carbon Emissions Reduction Target (CERT)	Requirement for energy suppliers to deliver carbon emissions reduction targets by promoting energy-efficiency improvements to households in Great Britain. Suppliers are expected to need to invest £3.2bn in meeting targets by the end of March 2011.
Energy Performance Certificates (EPCs)	Assessment of the energy efficiency of all buildings constructed, sold or let in the UK. EPCs include a list of recommendations for improving the level of energy efficiency achieved.

TOOL / MEASURE	DESCRIPTION
Standard Assessment Procedure (SAP)	Assessment of the energy efficiency of homes on a scale from 0 – 100, with 0 being very inefficient and 100 extremely efficient. The building regulations require a SAP assessment to be carried out for all new dwellings, conversions and refurbishments. It underpins the EPC.
National Home Energy Rating (NHER)	Another tool for assessing the energy efficiency of homes, on a scale of 0 – 20.
Display Energy Certificates	Analysis of the actual energy use of a building, required for all public buildings with a total useful floor area over 1,000m^2.[67]
Renewable Heat Incentive (RHI) (to be available from April 2011)	Payments for households, communities and businesses for getting their heat from renewable sources, whether on a large industrial scale, community heating or in the home. It will be funded by levies on suppliers of fossil fuels for heat. To be available from April 2011 across Great Britain.
Community Energy Saving Programme (CESP)	Obligation on energy suppliers and energy generators to work with local authorities and community organisations to deliver energy efficiency measures to around 90,000 homes across approximately 100 low-income areas across Great Britain.
Feed-in Tariffs (to be available from April 2010)	Feed-in tariff system, whereby it is proposed that small-scale producers (i.e. those producing up to 5 megawatts) will receive guaranteed payments for every kilowatt hour of renewable electricity they generate (the 'generation tariff') and export to the grid (the 'export tariff'). It is expected that this will be introduced in April 2010 and available across Great Britain.

[67]Public buildings are defined as buildings that are occupied by a public authority and institution providing a public service to a large number of persons and therefore visited by those persons.

Table 6: England and Wales

TOOL / MEASURE	DESCRIPTION
Climate Change Act 2008 Targets	Target to reduce CO_2 emissions by 80% below 1990 levels by 2050. Interim targets to reduce CO_2 emissions by 22% below 1990 levels by 2012, 28% by 2017 and 34% by 2022.
Zero Carbon Homes Target	Target for all new homes built from 2016 in England and Wales (subject to devolution of powers) to be zero carbon rated (NB this only applies to new build, not changes of use).
Proposed Home Energy Efficiency Target	Target for all homes to have received a 'whole house' energy package (including both energy saving and generation measures) with all lofts and cavity walls to be insulated by 2015 where practical (proposed in consultation of February 2009).
Part L of the Building Regulations	Sets energy efficiency standards for new build and certain categories of work to existing buildings, including extensions and conversions. Special considerations apply if work may adversely affect the appearance / character of a listed building.
Part G of the Building Regulations	Sets water efficiency standards for new build and certain categories of work to existing buildings, including extensions and conversions. Special considerations apply if work may adversely affect the appearance / character of a listed building.
Code for Sustainable Homes	Mandatory rating for all new homes built in England based on a scale of 0 – 6. All new social housing must meet level 3 at a minimum.

Table 7: Wales only

TOOL / MEASURE	DESCRIPTION
Welsh Assembly Government Greenhouse Gas Targets	Target to reduce greenhouse gas emissions by 3% per annum year on year in areas of devolved competence.
Welsh Assembly Government Renewables Targets	Targets for: • the installation of 100,000 micro-heating systems; • 200,000 micro-electricity systems; • 50 combined heat and power or district heating systems in Wales by 2050.

Table 8: Scotland only

TOOL / MEASURE	DESCRIPTION
Greenhouse Gas Emissions Targets	Target to reduce Scotland's greenhouse gas emissions by 80% by 2050, with an interim target of 42% by 2020.
Energy Targets	Targets: • for 20% of energy total energy use to come from renewable sources by 2020; • for 50% of gross electricity consumption to come from renewable sources by 2020, with 31% by 2011; • for 11% of heat demand to be met from renewable sources by 2020.
Scottish Planning Policy 6	Support for renewable energy through the planning system.

Table 9: Northern Ireland only

TOOL / MEASURE	DESCRIPTION
Emissions Reduction Target	Target to reduce emissions by 25% on 1990 levels by 2025.
Building Regulations Targets	Targets to improve the energy and carbon requirements of building regulations by 25 and 44% in 2010 and 2013 respectively, moving towards zero carbon thereafter.
Part F of the Building Regulations	Sets energy-efficiency standards for new build and certain categories of work to existing buildings, including extensions and conversions. Special considerations apply if work may adversely affect the appearance / character of a listed building.

APPENDIX C: Useful links

These are ordered by level of governance - from international to regional. Other tables are ordered alphabetically. These are all correct at the time of writing, but as external sources they may be subject to change.

Table 10: Governmental / statutory bodies

Organisation	Weblink	Activity
Intergovernmental Panel on Climate Change	www.ipcc.ch	Scientific body providing information on climate change
European Union	www.europa.eu	European policy and legislation
Build Up	www.buildup.eu/home	European portal on energy efficiency in buildings
Department of Energy and Climate Change	www.decc.gov.uk	UK policy on energy and climate change
Department for Environment, Food and Rural Affairs	www.defra.gov.uk	UK policy on the environment, food and rural affairs
Communities and Local Government	www.communities.gov.uk	UK policy on communities and local government (including planning and the Code for Sustainable Homes)
Department for Culture, Media and Sport	www.culture.gov.uk	UK policy on culture, media and sport (including heritage)
The Scottish Government	www.scotland.gov.uk	Policy in Scotland (including planning and the environment)
Welsh Assembly Government	www.wales.gov.uk	Policy in Wales (including planning and the environment)
Northern Ireland Executive	www.northernireland.gov.uk	Policy in Northern Ireland (including planning and the environment)
English Heritage	www.english-heritage.org.uk	The Government's statutory adviser on the historic environment in England
Historic Environment – Local Management	www.helm.org.uk	Programme established by English Heritage to provide information and advice about managing the historic environment

Organisation	Weblink	Activity
Cadw	www.cadw.wales.gov.uk	The Welsh Assembly Government's historic environment division
Historic Scotland	www.historic-scotland.gov.uk	Executive agency of the Scottish Government, dealing with the historic environment
Environment Agency	www.environment-agency.gov.uk	Executive non-departmental public body, dealing with the environment and sustainable development in the UK, particularly England and Wales
Scottish Environment Protection Agency	www.sepa.org.uk	Scotland's environmental regulator
Environment Agency (NI)	www.ni-environment.gov.uk	Agency within the Department of Environment in Northern Ireland, dealing with environmental policy and strategy
Natural England	www.naturalengland.org.uk	Independent public body dealing with England's natural environment
UK Planning Portal	www.planningportal.gov.uk	Planning portal for the UK
Homes and Communities Agency	www.homesandcommunities.co.uk	Housing and Regeneration Agency for England (including delivery of the Carbon Challenge programme)
Business Link	www.businesslink.gov.uk	Free business advice and support service (including on energy efficiency)
Act on CO_2 Campaign	www.direct.gov.uk/actonco2	Advice on saving money, energy and reducing CO_2 emissions
Help Wales reduce its carbon footprint campaign	www.wales.gov.uk	Advice on saving money, energy and reducing CO_2 emissions
Ofgem	www.ofgem.gov.uk	Regulator of the UK's gas and electricity networks (including issuing Levy Exemption Certificates)
Envirowise	www.envirowise.gov.uk	Advice for businesses on resource efficiency

Table 11: Organisations and schemes

Organisation	Weblink	Activity
Ancient Monuments Society	www.ancientmonumentssociety.org.uk	Statutory consultees for alterations for Scheduled Ancient Monuments and listed buildings of all periods
Association for the Conservation of Energy	www.ukace.org	Membership organisation to encourage awareness of, and investment in, energy conservation
Bat Conservation Trust	www.bats.org.uk	Umbrella organisation for the conservation of bats and their habitats
Biomass Energy Centre	www.biomassenergycentre.org.uk	Centre run by the UK Forestry Commission, providing advice on biomass (including information about suppliers)
British Hydropower Association	www.british-hydro.org	Membership organisation representing the interests of the UK hydropower industry
British Wind Energy Association	www.bwea.com	Trade and professional body for the UK wind and marine renewables industries
Building Research Establishment (BRE)	www.bre.co.uk www.breeam.org	Charity providing consultancy, testing and commissioned research services relating to the built environment. BRE is responsible for BREEAM environmental assessment methods, which are voluntary tools for assessing the environmental performance of various types of buildings on a scale ranging from 'pass' to 'outstanding'
Business in the Community	www.bitc.org.uk	Membership organisation and one of the Prince's Charities, helping businesses to tackle climate change

Organisation	Weblink	Activity
Carbon Reduction in Buildings	www.carb.org.uk	Research project aimed at reducing emissions from the UK building stock
Carbon Trust	www.carbontrust.co.uk	Independent company providing advice and support for businesses on saving energy
Centre for Alternative Technology	www.cat.org.uk	Centre providing education and information on environmental issues
Changeworks	www.changeworks.org.uk	Charity for improving quality of life and protecting the environment (including looking at energy in buildings)
Combined Heat and Power Association	www.chpa.co.uk	Membership organisation to promote the use of combined heat and power
Community Energy Scotland	www.communityenergyscotland.org.uk	Charity providing advice, funding and finance for community groups in Scotland
Constructing Excellence	www.constructingexcellence.org.uk	Membership organisation for driving change in the construction sector, including around sustainability
Council for British Archaeology	www.britarch.ac.uk	Educational charity dealing with archaeology. You should also contact the local planning authority for advice on local Archaeological Trusts.
Crichton Carbon Centre	www.carboncentre.org	Not-for-profit organisation conducting research and teaching in carbon management
Energy Efficiency Partnership for Homes	www.eeph.org.uk	Network for reducing the energy consumption by UK households
Energy Networks Association	www.energynetworks.org	Membership organisation for UK energy transmission and distribution. ENA provides information about Distribution Network Operators

Organisation	Weblink	Activity
Energy Saving Trust	www.energysavingtrust.org.uk	Non-profit organisation providing advice and support for householders on saving energy
Existing Homes Alliance	www.existinghomesalliance.org	Umbrella organisation calling for action to make existing homes fit for the 21st century
Garden History Society	www.gardenhistorysociety.org	Statutory consultee for alterations to registered parks and gardens
Georgian Group	www.georgiangroup.org.uk	Statutory consultee for listed buildings built between 1630 and 1840 and provider of advice on alterations
Green Tourism Business Scheme	www.green-tourism.co.uk	The national sustainable tourism certification scheme, offering accreditation to tourism businesses
Ground Source Heat Pump Association	www.gshp.org.uk	Membership organisation promoting the use of ground-source heat pumps
Institute of Historic Building Preservation	www.ihbc.org.uk	UK professional body for building conservation practitioners and historic environment experts
Micropower Council	www.micropower.co.uk	Membership organisation representing the microgeneration sector
National Energy Action	www.nea.org.uk	Campaign group for energy-efficient homes
National Non-Food Crops Centre	www.nnfcc.co.uk	Independent organisation providing advice on plant-based renewable materials and technologies
National Trust	www.nationaltrust.org.uk	Charity which protects historic properties, gardens, industrial monuments and mills and opens them to the public

Organisation	Weblink	Activity
The Prince's Foundation for the Built Environment	www.princes-foundation.org	Charity which teaches and practises timeless and ecological ways of planning, designing and building The Prince's Foundation for the Built Environment, in partnership with other organisations, is building an exemplar 'Natural House' using natural materials
The Prince's Regeneration Trust	www.princes-regeneration.org	Charity with dual objectives to conserve historic buildings and regenerate areas of social and economic need
Renewable Energy Association	www.r-e-a.net	Membership organisation representing renewable energy producers in the UK
Reuse It Yourself	www.reiy.net	Networks which collect and sell on excess construction materials
Royal Society for the Protection of Birds	www.rspb.org.uk	Charity to protect birds and the environment
Shrinking the Footprint	www.shrinkingthefootprint.cofe.anglican.org	The Church of England's national environmental campaign
Society for the Protection of Ancient Buildings	www.spab.org.uk	Charity dealing with all aspects of the survival of buildings which are old and interesting
Solar Trade Association	www.solar-trade.org.uk	Membership organisation representing business interests in the solar energy industry, and providing information and advice
Sustainable Energy Academy	www.sustainable-energyacademy.org.uk	Charity for reducing carbon footprint of buildings and communities
Theatres Trust	www.theatrestrust.org.uk	Statutory consultee for alterations to historic theatres of all periods
The Heritage Lottery Fund	www.hlf.org.uk	Funder of heritage projects, with information and advice on delivering successful projects

Organisation	Weblink	Activity
Twentieth Century Society	www.c20society.org.uk	Statutory consultee for listed buildings built from 1914 to the current time
UK Climate Impacts Programme (UKCIP)	www.ukcip.org.uk	Organisation helping other organisations to adapt to climate change
UK Green Buildings Council	www.ukgbc.org	Membership organisation to improve the sustainability of the built environment
UK Solar Energy Society	www.uk-ises.org	Non-profit organisation for advancing the use of solar energy
Victorian Society	www.victoriansociety.org.uk	Campaign group for the preservation of Victorian buildings, parks and gardens in England and Wales and statutory consultee for alterations to listed buildings built between 1840 and 1914. Provider of advice on alterations
Wood Energy Scotland	www.usewoodfuel.co.uk	Information on biomass in Scotland (including suppliers), run by the Forestry Commission Scotland
World Wildlife Fund	www.wwf.org.uk	Global environmental organisation. WWF is running the Great British Refurb campaign
Zero Carbon Hub	www.zerocarbonhub.org	Non-profit company coordinating the delivery of zero carbon homes

Table 12: Websites

Organisation	Weblink	Activity
British Geological Survey	www.bgs.ac.uk	Research organisation providing geological expertise and information
Centre for Ecology and Hydrology	www.ceh.ac.uk	Research organisation providing information on river flow rates
Electricity Info	www.electricityinfo.org	Information on the fuel sources used by UK power companies
Green Electricity	www.greenelectricity.org	Information on switching to green electricity
Pricerunner	www.pricerunner.co.uk	Site for comparing prices of different energy-efficient fixtures and fittings
Sutherland Tables	www.sutherlandtables.co.uk	Information about the cost of different fuels (by subscription)
Theatres Trust	www.theatrestrust.org.uk	Statutory consultee for alterations to historic theatres of all periods
Twentieth Century Society	www.c20society.org.uk	Statutory consultee for listed buildings built from 1914 to the current time
T-Zero	www.tzero.org.uk	Advice on sustainable refurbishment
Water Footprint	www.waterfootprint.org	Site for calculating water footprint

Table 13: Suppliers and products

Organisation	Weblink	Activity
Enhanced Capital Allowances Water Technologies List	www.eca-water.gov.uk	Information on approved water-saving technologies
Forest Stewardship Council (FSC)	www.fsc.org	Independent, not-for-profit organisation which promotes the responsible management of the world's forests through certification
Green Book Live	www.greenbooklive.com	Online database of environmental products and services
One Planet Products	www.oneplanetproducts.com	Non-profit organisation helping members to specify and purchase green construction materials
Programme for the Endorsement of Forest Certification schemes (PEFC)	www.pefc.org	Independent, not-for-profit organisation which promotes sustainably managed forests through certification
Real Assurance Scheme	www.realassurance.org.uk	Consumer code on microgeneration systems and a list of suppliers that have signed up to the code
Scottish Stone Liaison Group	www.sslg.co.uk	Membership organisation to promote the use of indigenous Scottish stone
Solar Keymark Certification Scheme	www.estif.org	Certification scheme for solar collectors and systems
UK Construction Product Association	www.constructionproducts.org.uk	Represents UK manufacturers and suppliers of construction products
UK Microgeneration Certification Scheme	www.microgenerationcertification.org	Independent certification scheme for microgeneration products and installers

APPENDIX D: Glossary

This glossary defines key terms used throughout the guide which may be unfamiliar or unclear. For definitions of specific planning terms, policies and legislation, please see Chapter 3 and Appendix B. For grants and financing arrangements, please see Appendix A.

Adaptation to climate change concerns ways to prepare for changes in climactic conditions; for example, expanding the size of gutters to deal with heavy downpours and storms.

Adaptations (environmental adaptations) are any alterations to the building which are intended to make it more environmentally sustainable (e.g. by saving energy, generating energy or adapting it to the impacts of climate change).

Biomass is the generation of energy through the combustion of organic materials, such as wood. Biomass boilers supply heat or hot water to buildings and usually run on woodchip, wood pellets or logs.

Breathability refers to the degree to which air is allowed to flow in and out of a building.

Brown energy is energy generated from non-renewable sources.

Building management systems enable the centralised control of temperatures and lighting in different parts of the building at different times.

Building regulations comprise the rules for how works to buildings may be carried out.

Carbon dioxide is the most common greenhouse gas and is often used as a measure of environmental impact (measured by tonne, which is around $550m^3$ of CO_2). Sometimes carbon is used as a measure instead.

Cold-bridging (thermal bridging) refers to localised areas which, without insulation, have higher thermal conductivity and so result in increased heat loss.

Combination boilers (combi boilers) act both as water-heating and central-heating boilers and therefore take up less space.

Combined heat and power plants burn fuels to produce both electricity and heat for use in buildings. Combined cooling, heat and power plants can be used to cool the building as well as heat it.

Condensing boilers are very efficient boilers, as they extract heat twice – the second time from flue gases that are wasted in conventional boilers.

Conservation area consent is permission required from the local planning authority to carry out substantial demolition of a structure within a conservation area.

Conservation areas are areas of special architectural or historic interest. This relates not only to the buildings themselves but to features of the area considered as a whole: for instance the layout of paths, roads and boundaries; or the way parks, gardens and greens are combined with the buildings. Conservation areas have special consideration under the planning system. They are usually designated by local authorities.

Double glazing is the insertion of two panes of glass into a window frame to reduce noise levels and heat loss.

Dynamic thermal simulation can be used to assess thermal mass, temperature and humidity readings.

Elevations (in relation to buildings) are the external surfaces of the building. The principal (or primary) elevation is the side of the building intended to be viewed most often – usually the front. Secondary elevations are the other sides of the building. Where a building is listed, the primary elevation tends to be the most sensitive.

Embodied energy is the energy consumed in extracting, processing, manufacturing, transporting and installing building materials or equipment, e.g. the energy used to fire bricks in kilns.

Fan pressure tests measure air leakage from a building.

Feasibility studies provide a thorough assessment of whether it would make sense to make certain environmental adaptations to particular buildings.

Financial payback is the length of time an initial outlay of money will be recouped through savings (e.g. on energy bills).

Flue is another word for a chimney to funnel exhaust air out of a building.

Fossil fuels are fuels which have been formed from the organic remains of plants or animals and include coal, oil and natural gas. They are non-renewable sources of energy.

Fuel poverty is the situation of households which need to spend over 10% of their income to heat the home to satisfactory levels (usually 21°C in the main living area and 18°C in other occupied rooms).

Geothermal energy is derived from heat stored deep below the surface of the earth and is normally used to provide electricity on a community-wide scale.

Green energy is energy generated from renewable sources.

Green roofs (sometimes known as sedum roofs) are roofs where plant life is encouraged, to help absorb CO_2 and promote biodiversity.

Greenhouse gases absorb heat from the sun and trap it in the lower atmosphere, causing an overall warming of the earth. The main greenhouse gases are carbon dioxide (CO_2), methane and nitrous oxide.

Grey water recycling is the collection of water which has already been used in a building (e.g. for washing) for re-use (e.g. for toilet flushing).

Heat pumps use heat from the air, the ground or water to provide a building with hot water or space heating (either directly or via the heating of water).

- *Air-source heat pumps* generate energy from the air outside the building.
- *Ground-source heat pumps* use the heat from the ground; they can be vertical (accessing the heat source through a deep borehole) or horizontal (using a shallow trench).
- *Water-source heat pumps* draw heat from water sources, such as lakes, springs or rivers.

Heat recovery systems use the heat from stale air leaving the building to heat fresh in-coming air, reducing the need for further heating of the building.

Hydroelectricity is electricity generated from the energy of flowing water, using hydroelectric turbines.

International Standard ISO 14001 is a standard that can be attained by companies operating with the highest environmental standards.

Kilowatt (kW) is a unit of power. One kilowatt is equal to 1000 watts. The number of kilowatts associated with an appliance or technology tells you how much energy can be produced at any point in time.

Kilowatt hour (kWh) is a unit of energy. One kilowatt hour is equal to the energy produced by a power of 1000 watts operating for 1 hour.
Using a 60 watt light bulb for an hour consumes 0.06 kilowatt hours of electricity. Using it for 1000 hours consumes 60 kilowatt hours.

Kilowatt peak (kWp) is a measure of power output, usually relating to solar PV when working under optimal conditions.

Lifetime tonnes of CO_2 are the tonnes of CO_2 emitted (or saved) over the expected lifetime of, for example, a building, appliance or energy-saving measure.

Listed building consent is permission required from the local planning authority for carrying out alterations to listed buildings (see Chapter 3 for more information).

Listed buildings are buildings with special architectural or historical interest. All buildings built before 1700 which survive in anything like their original condition are listed, as are most of those built between 1700 and 1840. Listed buildings have special consideration under the planning system. They are designated by the relevant national government.

Local planning authorities are the statutory bodies which are responsible for planning decisions. This is usually the district, unitary, city, borough, or metropolitan borough council. National Parks and Broads Authorities can also be local planning authorities.

Mechanical ventilation is the circulation of fresh air into, and through, a building by mechanical means, which therefore consumes some energy.

Mezzanine floors are extra levels in a building inserted between the original floor and ceiling to create more floor space.

Microgeneration is the generation of energy on a small scale, i.e. to meet some of the energy needs of a single building, or small set of buildings. Whilst generating energy at this scale does not deliver economies of scale associated with larger power plants, one efficiency benefit is that less energy is lost and wasted during transmission to the building.

Microrenewables are technologies which generate energy on a small scale from renewable sources, like the sun, wind or water.

Mitigation of climate change concerns reducing our emissions of greenhouse gases in order to avoid creating further global warming.

Natural ventilation is the circulation of fresh air into, and through, a building via breathable materials and the opening of windows and vents, rather than any mechanical means (although natural ventilation can be mechanically assisted, for example by the mechanical opening of roof vents when the building gets hot).

Operational energy is the energy required to run a building, once it is in use.

Passive solar gain refers to the entry of sunlight into parts of a building, allowing them to be heated and lighted naturally for much of the day.

Permitted development rights allow certain works to be carried out without planning permission (see Chapter 3 for more information).

Planning consent is permission required from the local planning authority to construct new buildings and carry out works to existing buildings (see Chapter 3 for more information).

Primary energy is raw fuel which has not been transformed or converted through any human-made process, e.g. coal, gas or sunlight.

Rainwater harvesting is the collection of rainwater for re-use (e.g. for toilet flushing, washing and watering gardens).

Relative humidity measures the moisture content of air. Museum exhibits often require control of relative humidity to between 50 and 60%.

Renewable energy is generated from natural resources, such as radiation from the sun, wind and water flow.

Resource efficiency is the efficient use of resources like water and energy. It can be achieved, for example, by reducing heat loss or water consumption in the building.

Reversibility concerns the ease with which alterations to the building can be undone in the future, returning the building to its original condition.

Scheduled monument consent is obtained from the national heritage agencies to carry out works to a scheduled ancient monument.

Secondary energy is energy which has been transformed or converted through a human-made process, for example electricity.

Secondary glazing is the addition of an extra window, or sheet of glass, behind an existing window to reduce noise levels and heat loss.

Smart meters / monitors provide information about how much energy is being used in the building at different times of day.

Solar photovoltaic (PV) cells use sunlight to supply electricity to a building. There are three main types of PV cells: polycrystalline, monocrystalline and amorphous silicon (thin film). The cells are arranged in arrays and can be mounted on the roof or the ground.

Solar thermal collectors use energy from sunlight to provide a building with hot water (and occasionally space heating). There are two main types of collector: evacuated tube and flat plate. They can be mounted on the roof or ground.

Stack effect / passive stack ventilation is the ventilation of a building through allowing air to be drawn through the building and displaced by cooler, fresher air from outside. It is associated with natural ventilation, rather than mechanical ventilation.

Sustainable development / sustainability is development that meets the needs of the present without compromising the ability of future generations to meet their own needs.

Sustainable urban drainage systems (SUDS) are systems which avoid flooding, pollution and damage to the environment in urban situations.

Thermal imaging maps differences in temperature, for example of different parts of a building.

Thermal mass measures the capacity of the building to store heat. It is determined by the thickness of the external walls and roof and the type of material used. So, for example, solid wall buildings made of stone and buildings with thatched roofs have a relatively higher thermal mass than timber-framed buildings or buildings with cavity walls.

Thermostats monitor and control temperature. Devices that are thermostatically controlled are switched on and off according to changes in temperature.

Traditional construction refers to a style of constructing buildings using solid walls and largely natural, breathable materials, to create a permeable fabric that allows moisture to be absorbed and released. Most listed buildings (and buildings constructed before the 1920s) are of traditional construction.

U-values measure how much heat will pass through one square metre of a structure when the air temperatures on either side differ by one degree. The U-value is expressed in watts per square metre per degree of temperature difference, so the lower the U-value the less energy is lost. For example, if a wall has a U-value of 1U, this means that 1 watt of power is lost per square metre, for every degree of temperature difference between the inside and the outside of the wall. So lower U-values represent less energy loss.

Wind energy is electricity generated from the energy of the wind, using wind turbines, which can be mounted on buildings or on the ground.

APPENDIX E: Bibliography

For websites consulted during the writing of this guide, please see the 'Useful links' section at Appendix C.
This was correct at the time of writing, but external sources may be subject to change.

A Stitch in Time,
The Society for the Protection of Ancient Buildings and the Institute of Historic Building Conservation, 2002. www.ihbc.org.uk

Adapting to Climate Change,
UK Climate Projections, Department for Environment, Food and Rural Affairs / Building Britain's Future / Act on CO_2, 2009. www.ukclimatechangeprojections.defra.gov.uk

Age Energy Research: A study of the energy usage of buildings relative to their age,
Jon Wallsgrove, 2007

Biomass Energy and the Historic Environment,
English Heritage, 2007. www.english-heritage.org.uk

Building Regulations and Historic Buildings: Balancing the needs for energy conservation with those of building conservation: an interim guidance note on the application of part L,
English Heritage, 2002. www.english-heritage.org.uk

Buyer's Guide to a Greener Home,
Sponge, 2008. www.spongenet.org

Carbon Countdown for Homes,
World Wildlife Fund, 2008. www.wwf.org.uk

Climate Change and the Historic Environment,
English Heritage, 2008. www.english-heritage.org.uk

Climate Change and the Historic Environment,
University College London, 2005. http://eprints.ucl.ac.uk/2082

Conservation Bulletin 57: Adapting to a Changing Climate,
English Heritage, 2008. www.english-heritage.org.uk

Cutting Down on Carbon – Improving the energy efficiency of historic buildings,
English Heritage, 2007. www.english-heritage.org.uk

Eco-Refurbishment and the Historic Environment,
Bristol City Council. www.bristol.gov.uk

Energy Conservation in Historic Houses: A guide for historic house owners,
Smiths Gore, 2009. www.smithsgore.co.uk

Energy Conservation in Traditional Buildings,
English Heritage, 2007. www.english-heritage.org.uk

Energy Efficiency in Refurbishment,
CIBSE, 2003

Energy Heritage: A guide to energy efficiency in traditional and historic homes,
Changeworks, 2008. www.changeworks.org.uk

Energy Modelling in Traditional Scottish Houses,
Historic Scotland Technical Group, 2008. www.historic-scotland.gov.uk

Energy Performance Certificates and Non-Dwellings: A guide for building owners, landlords and tenants,
HM Government, 2008. www.communities.gov.uk

Energy Performance Certificates for Historic and Traditional Homes,
English Heritage, 2007. www.english-heritage.org.uk

Evaluation of the Scottish Renewables Heating Pilot,
Scottish Government Social Research, 2008. www.scotland.gov.uk

Feasibility Study on Torr Vale Mill,
Roger Hannah and Company, April 2009

Flooding and Historic Buildings: Technical Advice Note,
English Heritage, 2004. www.english-heritage.org.uk

Future Water: The Government's Water Strategy for England,
Department for Environment, Food and Rural Affairs, February 2008. www.defra.gov.uk

Heat and Energy Saving Strategy Consultation,
Department of Energy and Climate Change, February 2009. www.decc.gov.uk

Heritage and Culture: Energy saving in historic sites and modern buildings,
The Carbon Trust, 2007. www.carbontrust.co.uk

Heritage Counts 2008,
English Heritage, 2008. www.english-heritage.org.uk

Improving the Thermal Performance of Traditional Windows,
Historic Scotland / Glasgow Caledonian University / English Heritage, 2008. www.historic-scotland.gov.uk

Inform Guide – Energy efficiency in traditional homes,
Historic Scotland, 2008. www.historic-scotland.gov.uk

Lose or Re-use: Managing heritage sustainably,
Lydia Wilson, 2007. www.uahs.org.uk

Low Carbon Existing Homes,
UK Green Building Council, 2008. www.ukgbc.org

Low Carbon Homes: Towards zero carbon refurbishment feasibility study,
Energy for Sustainable Development, 2004. www.generationhomes.co.uk

Micro Wind Generation and Traditional Buildings,
English Heritage, 2007. www.english-heritage.org.uk

Microgeneration in the Historic Environment,
English Heritage, 2008. www.helm.org.uk

New Tricks with Old Bricks,
Empty Homes Agency, 2008. www.emptyhomes.com

Office of Climate Change Household Emissions Project,
Office of Climate Change, 2007. www.occ.gov.uk

Planning Greener Heritage Projects,
The Heritage Lottery Fund, 2009. www.hlf.org.uk

Renewable Heritage: A guide to microgeneration in traditional and historic homes,
Changeworks, 2009. www.changeworks.org.uk

Retrofitting Soho: Improving the sustainability of historic core areas,
The Max Lock Centre, University of Westminster, 2008. www.westminsterresearch.wmin.ac.uk

Roof Renovation – listed building experiences,
Green Building Magazine, Richard Oxley, 2007

Small Scale Solar Electric (Photovoltaic) Energy and Traditional Buildings,
English Heritage, 2008. www.english-heritage.org.uk

Small Scale Solar Thermal Energy and Traditional Buildings,
English Heritage, 2008. www.english-heritage.org.uk

Sustainability Brief (version 2),
British Land, 2007. www.britishland.com/responsibility

Sustainable Energy – Without the Hot Air,
David MacKay, 2009. www.withouthotair.com

The Ampere Strikes Back,
Energy Saving Trust, July 2007.
www.energysavingtrust.org.uk

The Environmental Handbook,
Feilden Clegg Bradley, 2007.

The Good Maintenance Guide,
The Society for the Protection of Ancient Buildings, 2008.

The Whole House Book,
Cindy Harris and Pat Borer, CAT Publications, 2008.

Thermal Mass Energy Savings Potential in Residential Buildings,
J. Kosny, T. Petrie, D. Gawin, P. Childs, A. Desjarlais, and J.Christian, Buildings Technology Center, ORNL, 2001.
www.ornl,gov

Thermal Mass Sustainable Energy INFO fact sheet,
Sustainable Energy Authority, Victoria.
ww.sustainability.vic.gov.au

The Scottish Renewable Heating Pilot – An operational perspective,
Energy Saving Trust, 2008.
www.energysavingtrust.org.uk

The UK Low Carbon Transition Plan: National strategy for climate and energy,
HM Government, 2009. www.decc.gov.uk

Transforming Existing Buildings: The Green Challenge: Final report,
Cyril Sweett on behalf of the Royal Institution of Chartered Surveyors, 2007.

Upgrading Energy Conservation in Historic Buildings: A case study of a holistic approach,
Richard Oxley, Peter Warm and Mary Craig, on behalf of the National Trust, 2004.

Value Added: the economic, social and environmental benefits from creating incentives for the repair, maintenance and use of historic buildings,
The Prince's Regeneration Trust, 2007.
www.princes-regeneration.org

Why Waste Heat?,
Institution of Civil Engineers, 2009. www.ice.org.uk

Wind Energy and the Historic Environment,
English Heritage, 2005. www.english-heritage.org.uk

APPENDIX F: Index

Acknowledgements
This guide was produced with invaluable contributions from individuals with experience of adapting listed or historic buildings to improve environmental sustainability. In particular:

The Prince's Regeneration Trust is grateful to all those who provided case studies (and who are acknowledged accordingly in the guide).

We would also like to thank those who gave up their time to provide advice, meet us or organise site visits, in particular Moray Glennie of Hillcrest Housing Association, Terry Eccles at the London Transport Museum and the various members of staff at The National Trust.

We are particularly grateful for the help of colleagues in the final proofing and editing of the guide, especially Caroline Cattini from English Heritage, Susan Lawson from Alan Baxter & Associates, Ian Morrison at The Heritage Lottery Fund, Helen Drury from the Department of Energy and Climate Change, David Balcombe of The Green Edge Ltd, who also led us on a site visit and Dermot MacRandal at the Northern Ireland Environment Agency.

Thanks also go to Jen Grindley, who volunteered at The Prince's Regeneration Trust, for her help in preparing the final document.

We would like to thank Alan Baxter & Associates for kindly hosting the launch of this guide and the Heritage of London Trust for supporting this publication.

Finally, from all the staff at the Prince's Regeneration Trust, we would like to acknowledge the tremendous time and effort given to this project by Sarah Fisher, while she was on secondment from the Department for Environment, Food and Rural Affairs.

This comprehensive practical guide brings together advice on tackling climate change through the refurbishment and conversion of all types of listed buildings in the UK. Although the focus is on listed buildings, it applies equally to buildings in conservation areas, and in many cases, to other unlisted historic buildings.

'The Green Guide for Historic Buildings' is unique in that it covers all types of historic buildings, from industrial buildings to inner city flats; it is relevant for buildings across the UK; it is accessible for all and requires no previous knowledge or expertise; and uses best practice case studies to illustrate the advice.

It includes solutions for saving energy and generating it from renewable sources, whilst conserving the significance of the building; it explains how to proceed with the work, including obtaining statutory permissions and funding, finding suppliers and knowing what questions to ask.

The Prince's Regeneration Trust wishes to acknowledge the support of our sponsors who have funded this publication, including the Heritage of London Trust.

The cover shows: the Power House at Gunpowder Mill; Denton Hall; Yorkshire Field Barns; and The Natural History Museum. Photographs are reproduced permission of: The Hill Group; NG Bailey; Feilden Clegg Bradley Studios; and The Natural History Museum respectively.

Email:
info@princes-regeneration.org

Web:
www.princes-regeneration.org

THE PRINCE'S CHARITIES

THE PRINCE'S REGENERATION TRUST

Heritage of London Trust

TSO
Information & publishing solutions

www.tso.co.uk

ISBN 978-0-11-706844-5